COST
MANAGEMENT
for Today's Advanced Manufacturing

COST
MANAGEMENT
for Today's Advanced Manufacturing
THE CAM-I CONCEPTUAL DESIGN

Edited by
Callie Berliner
and James A. Brimson

HARVARD BUSINESS SCHOOL PRESS
Boston, Massachusetts

Library of Congress Cataloging-in-Publication Data

Cost management for today's advanced manufacturing : the CAM-I
   conceptual design / edited by Callie Berliner and James A. Brimson.
      p.   cm.
   Includes index.
   ISBN 0-87584-197-X
   1. Costs, Industrial.   2. Computer integrated manufacturing
systems—Costs.   I. Berliner, Callie, 1955–   .   II. Brimson, James
A., 1947–   .
TS167.C67 1988
658.1'55—dc19   88-10959
                                                                                      CIP

CONTENTS

PREFACE

During the past several years there has been an increasing need for a systematic study to define the role of cost management in an advanced manufacturing environment. In order to remain competitive internationally, companies have steadily adopted new technologies, such as material-requirements planning, computer-aided design, just-in-time, robotics, and others. However, during this period of change, management and financial systems have remained essentially unaltered. As a consequence, many companies are struggling with important economic issues, such as how to cost-justify capital investments, how to improve product cost information, how to change decision-support tools like product-abandonment models and make/buy decisions, and how to revise performance measures that currently encourage only short-term productivity.

In 1986, Computer Aided Manufacturing-International, Inc. (CAM-I) formed a consortium of progressive industrial organizations, professional accounting firms, and government agencies to define the role of cost management in the new environment. The goal of the coalition was to provide an international forum where cost management experts could share ideas and experiences and consolidate their knowledge about practices that have proved successful in an automated environment. Through this interaction, the group has unified approaches to cost management and encouraged implementation of new ideas.

The consortium identified three phases for study, each phase to last approximately one year:

- Phase I (1986): Conceptual Design
- Phase II (1987): Systems Design
- Phase III (1988): Implementation

PHASE I (1986): CONCEPTUAL DESIGN

The final product of this phase consisted of a review of current cost management practices to assess the state-of-the-art, and the development of a Cost Management System (CMS) Conceptual Design.

The state-of-the-art review was conducted as a joint research project funded by CAM-I and the National Association of Accountants (NAA). This study, entitled *Management Accounting in the New Manufacturing Environment,* is available through the NAA. This book, *Cost Management for Today's Advanced Manufacturing,* was developed by the CMS sponsors under the guidance of CAM-I. The development of the text drew on the experience of experts within the sponsor organizations, supplemented as needed by outside sources.

PHASE II (1987): SYSTEMS DESIGN

The objective of this phase was to provide each sponsor company with a systems architecture of cost management as defined during Phase I. Key concepts like non-value-added costs, activity accounting, technology accounting, and improved traceability of manufacturing costs were addressed. Design implications resulting from the transition from labor-based production to just-in-time (JIT), islands of automation, and computer-integrated manufacturing (CIM) were considered. System modules were defined as to their features, functions, and interfaces. New data elements, both financial and nonfinancial, and key report formats were defined. In addition, several concepts from the Phase I Conceptual Design were expanded through the development of research papers. Topics addressed included target costing, cost drivers and their causal relations, portfolio management of investment opportunities, and an evaluation of current manufacturing decision-making tools for make/buy and offshore sourcing.

CAM-I compiled these data into a Cost Management System Document to provide each company's management with a guide as to how the Conceptual Design principles can be addressed in a system.

PHASE III (1988): IMPLEMENTATION

The objective of Phase III is to demonstrate the cost management principles. Topics considered are as follows:

- Development of strategies to implement the Phase II design, including migration from current to new, and module-implementation strategy for different environments
- Pilot implementation
- Identification of knowledge lacunae and areas requiring further research
- Reporting of implementation experiences
- Methods for influencing change in the cost accounting standards and regulations, as required, of the Department of Defense, the Internal Revenue Service, and the Securities and Exchange Commission

Implementation issues as they apply to existing systems and the impact on the organization are covered.

ACKNOWLEDGMENTS

The cost management concepts condensed in this book represent the cumulative experience of the sponsors, who are some of the largest and most successful companies in the United States and Europe. These firms employ the best of Western business practices, since they are willing to break new ground and develop fresh approaches to the challenges provided by new technology.

The Conceptual Design group identified four dimensions of the cost management problem: manufacturing practices, accounting models and practices, performance measurements, and investment management. Chapters in this book correspond to these areas. Four committees were formed, and committee chairmen were elected and given the responsibility of coordinating the efforts of their colleagues. These committee chairmen deserve special mention: Norm Raffish, Deloitte, Haskins & Sells, manufacturing practices; John T. Wells, Arthur Young & Company, accounting models and practices; Lawrence J. Utzig, General Electric Company, performance measurements; Rande Wagner, General Dynamics, investment management.

Also deserving special recognition is Tony Isaac, The Plessey Company plc, who chaired the European Life-Cycle Management Committee.

Finally, an Executive Committee consisting of senior-level management representatives from each sponsor organization was formed to provide overall guidance and direction to the project. Their input and support ensured that the Conceptual Design would focus on issues of prime importance to upper management. The Phase I sponsor organizations were the following:

SPONSOR COMPANIES	KEY REPRESENTATIVES	EXECUTIVE COMMITTEE
Allied Signal Automotive Sector	G. R. Papp Thomas C. Seelig	

SPONSOR COMPANIES	KEY REPRESENTATIVES	EXECUTIVE COMMITTEE
Allison Gas Turbine Division General Motors Corporation	Bob Grande Falus C. Polston	
Arthur Andersen & Company	Steven M. Hronec	Steven M. Hronec
Arthur Young & Company	John T. Wells, Jr.	Thomas Gunn
Boeing Military Aircraft Company	Joe D. Hawkins	James S. Niederkrome
British Aerospace plc	David Walker	
Coopers & Lybrand	R. J. Davies Henry J. Johansson J. Pendlebury J. Stark	Henry J. Johansson
Deloitte Haskins & Sells	Joel Kaplan Norm Raffish Ralph Randall	Ralph Randall
Eastman Kodak Company	Richard Dickerson	
Eaton Corporation	Brock Hattox	Brock Hattox
Ernst & Whinney	N. F. R. Carratu John G. Kammlade Robert McIlhattan G. Tunley	Paul F. McMahon
Garrett Turbine Engine	Jack L. Gorman Larry D. Hawkins Douglas K. Krieg Ron Utke	
General Dynamics/ Fort Worth	R. G. Wagner Van Ables	

SPONSOR COMPANIES	KEY REPRESENTATIVES	EXECUTIVE COMMITTEE
General Electric Company	Harry B. Howe Lawrence J. Utzig	Thomas O'Brien
Grumman Corporation	Mark DiFilippo Frank Kratochvil Douglas H. Rennie Brad Scheiner Aglaia Stalb	Mark DiFilippo
GTE Government Systems, Inc.	John DeBaie Frederick K. Larson	Ronald Gordon
Harsco Corporation/ BMY Division	Kenneth L. Newberry	Bruce Forinash
Hughes Aircraft Company	Marsha A. Carter Jose Garcia Landriz	
International Computers, Ltd.	R. Powell Paul Reeves	
ITT-AMT Center	Reinhart Sanders Armand Wielockx	
Lockheed Aeronautical Systems Co., California	Gunnar M. Haase	Guss Andres
Lockheed Aeronautical Systems Co., Georgia	Howell K. Teasley	V. Herbert Brady
Lockheed Missiles & Space Co., Inc.	Carolyn R. McGrath	V. M. Glick
Martin Marietta Energy Systems, Inc.	F. F. Carringer Dick Fletcher Donna J. Jones Ron Ragland	

SPONSOR COMPANIES	KEY REPRESENTATIVES	EXECUTIVE COMMITTEE
McDonnell Douglas Corporation	C. B. Caudill David O. Jackson	Don J. Homan
Motorola, Inc.	Tom Pryor Dave Tobiasz	
Peat, Marwick, Main & Company	Thomas W. Buesing Michael Jeans Dan Johnson Ed Lighthiser Richard B. Troxel	Richard B. Troxel
The Plessey Company plc	Steve Bramhall J. Gargaro Richard Goddard Tony Isaac	Tony Isaac
Pratt & Whitney Aircraft Company	John R. McGraw, Jr.	Mark Coran
Price Waterhouse	Robert G. Eiler Mike Grady Allen Wizdo	Robert G. Eiler
RHP Industrial Bearings, Ltd.	Ian Galloway P. H. Stevenson	
Rockwell International Corporation	Frank L. O'Reilly J. K. Schubert	J. K. Schubert
TRW, Inc.	William Kelly Catherine B. Steger	Dick Mulligan
U.S. Air Force AFWAL/ MLTC	Donn Aaby Rein Abel John S. Adams Michael Bindner Dennis Drouillard Raymond D. Inglin Brian A. Kosmal Neal Rappaport Michael J. Reed Edward M. Rogers J. H. Stolorow	Brigadier General John D. Slinkard

SPONSOR COMPANIES	KEY REPRESENTATIVES	EXECUTIVE COMMITTEE
U.S. Department of Energy	Bill Cleland	
U.S. Navy	Robert E. Achenbach	
	Harry S. Bagley	
	Domenic C. Cipicchio	
	Stephen F. Weber	
Westinghouse Electric Corporation	James H. Allen	
	George A. Beserock III	
	Richard L. Engwall	
Williams International	Leonard D. Frescoln	
	John K. Mulligan	

The support and input provided by our university affiliates has contributed greatly to the development of the Conceptual Design. From the beginning of the project CAM-I has placed a high priority on the active involvement of university professors. They have provided ideas and guidance which have been embedded in the concepts of the design. In particular, we would like to thank George Foster, Robert S. Kaplan, and Robin Cooper for the significant amount of time they have devoted to working with the CAM-I staff and the sponsor organizations. Their insights have had a profound impact on the direction of the project.

UNIVERSITY AFFILIATES	UNIVERSITY REVIEW PANEL
George Foster, Stanford University	Michael C. Burstein, Industrial Technology Institute
Robert S. Kaplan, Harvard University	Bernard Coda, North Texas State University
Jeffrey Miller, Boston University	Robin Cooper, Harvard University
Wickham Skinner, Harvard University	Bela Gold, Claremont College
	Anthony G. Hopwood, London School of Economics
	Dan Shunk, Arizona State University
	William G. Sullivan, University of Tennessee
	Gerry Susman, Pennsylvania State University

Several professional societies were involved in the project. Al King and Patrick Romano of the National Association of Accountants (NAA) were strong supporters of CMS from the beginning. Their enthusiasm has been demonstrated by the jointly funded NAA/CAM-I research project, which provided background information for the Conceptual Design. Throughout the project the NAA has been an excellent partner in this endeavor. Christian van Schayk of the American Society of Mechanical Engineers (ASME) worked closely with the manufacturing practices committee, providing valuable insights about the role of design engineers in cost management. The American Association of Accountants (AAA), via Fredric Jacobs of Michigan State University and Ralph Estes of Wichita State University, annotated sections of the Conceptual Design with further references. The participation of these professional societies resulted in a document that addresses the needs of a wider audience than our program sponsors.

Synthesizing the approaches of many diverse organizations and individuals required a special set of skills. Special recognition should be given to Gary Gollobin, who was the project manager during Phase I and Tom Pryor, project manager for Phases II and III. Callie Berliner helped write and edit a large portion of this book. In particular, her efforts in interfacing with the sponsors during the review process greatly enhanced the Conceptual Design. The CAM-I staff in Poole, England, coordinated the European CMS activities under the direction of Frank Davenport. Finally, the work could not have been completed without the administrative skills of Sandy Shoop, who kept us all on track. My thanks to all of these people.

Arlington, Texas   *James A. Brimson*
March 1988   *CMS Project Director*

COST
MANAGEMENT
for Today's Advanced Manufacturing

CHAPTER 1

CMS Conceptual Design

T his chapter summarizes the design of the CAM-I Cost Management System (CMS). It states the CMS key concepts, objectives, and guiding principles.

Advanced manufacturing technologies, such as robotics, computer-aided design (CAD), and flexible manufacturing systems (FMS), have revolutionized the manufacturing shop floor. They have dramatically changed manufacturing cost-behavior patterns: the direct labor and inventory components of product cost are decreasing, while depreciation, engineering, and data-processing costs are increasing. These changes have resulted in higher overhead rates and a shrinking base of labor over which to allocate those costs.

The new technologies have shaken the foundation of how companies account for costs. Management can no longer accept an environment where cost accounting contributes to overhead rates so high as to obscure true product cost, where the impact of work-in-process (WIP) on product cost is hidden in numerous cost categories, and where other accounting practices hinder manufacturing.

At the same time, international competition has become more vigorous. Foreign competition, particularly from the Far East, has increased its market share by improving product quality and reducing costs (by eliminating waste). These changes emphasize the need for manufacturing excellence. For many companies, the stake is survival. Managers need up-to-date, concise information, formatted to assist them in making the right decisions. Cost management systems, therefore, must provide the cost information necessary for informed operational and strategic decisions about resource acquisition and use.

Most manufacturing managers know about these problems. What they do not know is which cost management practices will be successful in an automated manufacturing environment. To be sure, fragments of this knowledge have been developed by various sources. Still, there is no comprehensive knowledge base of cost management strategies for computer-integrated manufacturing (CIM). Today's managers are making decisions in complex, technology-driven situations where the information supplied by their internal management systems is inadequate and often misleading.

Existing cost accounting systems and cost management practices do not adequately support the objectives of automated manufacturing. They are plagued by high overhead rates resulting from inadequately traced costs, and they do not pinpoint the activities that generate unnecessary costs rather than customer-perceived value. Current systems and practices do not penalize overproduction; in fact, the philosophy of absorbing overhead costs by allocating them on the basis of production volume encourages excess inventories.

At present, the cost of quality deficiencies in products or processes are not adequately identified or reported. Rather than identifying significant costs at the design and development phases of a product's life cycle, management focuses on controlling the production process. Current cost accounting and cost management practices do not support justification of new investments in advanced manufacturing technology: they fail to monitor the benefits obtained. They employ performance measurements that often conflict with strategic manufacturing objectives, and they cannot adequately evaluate the importance of nonfinancial measures such as quality, throughput, and flexibility.

Progressive industrial organizations on the leading edge of automation have joined professional accounting companies, government agencies, and universities in a coalition organized and managed by CAM-I. The goal of the coalition is to build a common knowledge base of cost management practices by creating an international forum for cost management experts to share ideas and experiences, and by providing a mechanism for the consolidation of the pooled knowledge. The remainder of this chapter describes the key assumptions, features, concepts, and principles upon which the CMS Conceptual Design is based.

It must be stressed that this book presents only the preliminary findings of the consortium. Much work is still needed to translate the concepts into a cost management system that will assist a company in upgrading or replacing its existing cost systems. Future tasks are to develop key concepts further; develop a computer-based model to simulate the impact of implementing CMS principles; translate CMS concepts into a high-level systems specification for implementing new cost management systems; and create implementation guidelines.

Several leading-edge companies are now creating prototype systems that address certain CMS principles. These initial efforts are the beginnings of a data-processing solution to the inadequacies of current cost management practices. The experience gained will form the kernel of a full-scale, up-to-date cost management system.

KEY CONCEPTS

There are several fundamental differences between existing cost accounting systems and the CMS Conceptual Design. Cost management is more comprehensive than cost accounting. While cost accounting takes a historical perspective and focuses on reporting costs, cost management takes a proactive role in planning, managing, and reducing costs. This does not imply that there will be no need to report actual results. Because conditions change between the planning and execution, a feedback loop must work to modify the plan to improve execution. Some of the more important advantages of CMS over traditional practices are the following:

- Continual improvement in eliminating non-value-added costs
- Activity accounting
- Externally driven targets, including target cost
- Improved traceability of costs to management reporting objectives

Eliminating Non-Value-Added Costs

Recent experiences of manufacturers have reinforced the idea that the successful company will be one that has made a firm commitment to eliminating waste. In a manufacturing process certain activities add no value, as seen by consumers. They result in the profitless spending of time, money, and resources and add unnecessary cost to the product. A non-value-added activity is an activity that can be eliminated with no deterioration of product attributes (performance, function, quality, perceived value).

The concept of non-value-added can be visualized easily in production-related activities: value is only being added to a product when it is being processed. Products sitting idle in a manufacturing plant cause costs to be incurred without improving the product. Such costs include inventory carrying, storage, expediting, and production control. Many of these costs could be eliminated by restructuring the manufacturing process to keep the product flowing continuously through the facility. The resulting product will be at least identical, if not superior, yet it will cost less. One way of looking at this is by breaking the process lead time into its four components:

$$\text{Lead time} = \text{Process time} + \text{Inspection time} + \text{Move time} + \text{Wait time}$$

Move time, inspection time, and wait time represent non-value-added time, since the product is not being processed. The lead-time equation, therefore, can be restated as

$$\text{Lead time} = \text{Process time} + \text{Non-value-added time}$$

Under this concept, manufacturing-cycle efficiency (MCE) can be computed as:

$$\text{MCE} = \frac{\text{Processing time}}{\text{Processing time} + \text{Inspection time} + \text{Wait time} + \text{Move time}}$$

In many manufacturing companies today, the MCE is often less than 10 percent. In an optimized manufacturing environment MCE would be 1 (100 percent), since the goal is to eliminate non-value-added time by producing the exact needs at the exact time at every stage of production (see Figure 1.1). To achieve an MCE of 1 would require reducing inspection time, wait time, and move time to zero. This perfect flow would occur only if the following conditions were met:

Lot size = 1
Time between operations = 0
Defects = 0
Setup time = 0
Operations perfectly balanced
Minimum work-in-process (WIP) inventory (parts in machine)
Parts never sit

Figure 1.1
Lead-Time Reduction

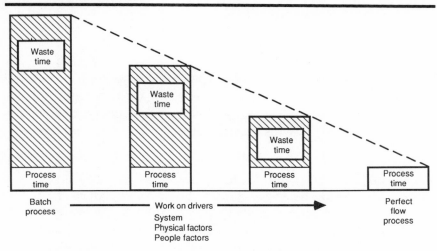

Source: *Lawrence J. Utzig, General Electric Company.*

The non-value-added concept is also useful in analyzing process time. An idle process is not generating revenue. A manufacturing process can be idle for any of the following reasons:

PROCESS-TIME LOSSES	REASONS
Downtime	Equipment failure, setups, adjustments
Speed	Idling and minor stoppages
	Reduced speed
Quality problems	Defects in process
	Defective material
Balanced production	Unbalanced production (bottlenecks)
	Failures in other processes
Orders	Insufficient orders
	Idle shifts

When applied to support functions, the concept of non-value-added relates to unnecessary or ineffective activities. Support functions such as strategic planning, product/process development, purchasing, and finance may never be directly involved with physically processing the product, yet they have a major impact on product revenue and costs.

Activity Accounting

A company executes its business objectives through the activities performed by each specialized group in the organization. Activity accounting is the collection of financial and operational performance information about significant activities of the business.

Functions, Activities, and Tasks. A function is a group of activities having a common objective within the business. For example, the function of physically manufacturing a product consists of a finite set of individual activities that change the shape of material, machine parts to a fixed dimension, obtain a surface finish, and assemble the parts or materials. A functional view is often significantly different from an organizational one, since its purpose is to identify homogeneous activities. Organization units are often established on such factors as managerial talents and product lines.

The functions defined by the CMS Engineering/Manufacturing Functional Model (see Chapter 3) are practiced by all discrete parts manufacturers, although the importance of each function varies by company and industry. For example, all companies require a product design in order to manufacture the product. In some industries the product design may be developed by the customer. At some companies the product design may be done internally and account for 15–20 percent of the product cost, while in other industries it may be less than 1 percent.

Functions can be decomposed into processes that represent the ongoing sets of activities. Activities are those actions needed to achieve the goals and objectives of the function. Under this definition, manufacturing processes would be considered activities: for example, machining, heat-treating, and assembly. Activities can be defined in terms of the information elements necessary to perform the activity and to create the output.

Activities can be decomposed into tasks, subtasks, and operations. Tasks are the work elements of an activity. The relation between functions, activities, and tasks can be described as follows:

Function	Perform manufacturing
Activity	Machine small parts
	for sheet-metal center
Task	Drill holes
Information element	Work order
	Process plan

Part number

Although there are hierarchical relations between functions, activities, and tasks, the term *activity* will be used in a general sense to stand for all of them. The function level is often too global to provide accurate traceability, and tasks are often too small (localized) a detail for control. For this reason, activities in the CMS Functional Model were chosen to document the operations of the organization.

Advantages of Activity Accounting. The CMS Conceptual Design incorporates the idea that costs are incurred through a firm's activities. For example, a customer order will trigger a series of activities from marketing through purchasing, production control, manufacturing, and shipping, all of which are required to make and deliver the product.

However, an entirely different set of activities exists to ensure the ongoing viability of the company. Many of the activities of design engineering and other units are focused on the firm's future needs. The costs associated with these activities represent a company's investment in the future and should be matched to the life-cycle costs of both products and processes.

Activity accounting is the basis of the CMS Conceptual Design, since it provides a natural baseline for describing a manufacturing process; a common denominator among cost accounting, performance measurement, and investment management; and the visibility of non-value-added activities.

Activities are "natural" identifiers, since they are easily understood by such diverse groups as engineers, manufacturers, financial personnel, and top management. They are easily understood because they correspond to familiar terms and events that occur in manufacturing. Today, much accounting information is presented in terms of finance rather than terms users can understand. For example, when overhead is charged to products using a predetermined rate, most users do not understand what comprises the charge and cannot relate it to the activities and tasks they perform. As a result, they often distrust the fairness of the charge and feel they have little information to control that cost.

Another advantage of activity accounting is that it is conceptually easy to associate cost and performance data with an activity. The cost of performing an activity is the sum of the direct labor, direct material, direct technology, other directly traceable costs, and overhead. The time required for performing an activity can be expressed as time devoted to an activity and the elapsed time. Transactions are often associated with activities. They are defined as physical (including electronic) documents associated with activities that impact information. In a purchasing department the following transactions can be associated with activities:

ACTIVITY	TRANSACTION
Identify requirement	Purchase requisition
Place order	Purchase order

Activities are a common denominator among cost accounting, performance measurement, and investment management. Activity accounting provides a logical framework for integrating these three critical areas, which in today's systems are often independent. If the functions remain independent, each seeks to optimize its own objectives, resulting in less-than-optimal performance by the business as a whole.

Cost accounting can be viewed as identifying the cost of performing significant activities of the business. The goal of performance measurement is to determine the efficiency and effectiveness of activities. The purpose of investment management is to identify, evaluate, and implement new activities, or alternatives for performing existing ones, to improve the future performance of the firm.

Activities also provide a basis for understanding the cost of performance drivers. A driver is an activity or condition that has a direct influence on the operational performance and cost structure, or both, of other activities. There are hierarchies of activities that cause other activities to occur.

A common misunderstanding regarding activities is that a tremendous level of detail is needed to account for them. But the CMS Conceptual Design proposes to capture and track cost and performance data for only those few *significant* activities that constitute the bulk of the total work within any organization.

Target Cost

Target cost represents a market-based cost that is calculated using a sales price necessary to capture a predetermined market share. In competitive industries a unit sales price would be established independent of the initial product cost. If the target cost is below the initial forecast of product cost, the company must drive the unit cost down over a designated period to compete.

Target cost = Sales price (for the target market share)
− Desired profit

If the target cost is initially lower than the budgeted or standard costs, cost reductions would be factored into the budget and standards over a period of time. Cost reduction can be achieved in two ways: (1) A learning curve occurs during early production volumes as a process is being refined. (2) The company applies a philosophy of continual improvement in eliminating waste.

To implement the target cost concept, a company may want to develop more detailed measurement systems for activity-level costs and performance. Such systems would help identify progress in meeting the overall target cost objectives.

Improved Traceability of Costs to Management Reporting Objectives

The usefulness of cost information is directly related to the accurate traceability of costs to the management reporting objectives. Inaccurate and global allocations of costs based on inappropriate assumptions regarding cost-behavior patterns and cause-and-effect relations distort information and lead to poor decisions.

Automation significantly alters the cost-behavior patterns and materiality of technology costs: it leads to a higher percentage of fixed cost because of its capital-intensity. Higher ratios of fixed costs (automation) to variable costs (labor) require better traceability of costs. In the most extreme case (a "lights out" factory) all significant costs except materials will be considered fixed. In such an environment little insight is gained through analyzing the fixed-variable relation. Instead, direct traceability becomes paramount. Improved traceability is achieved by determining the cause-and-effect relations between activities and such management reporting objectives as product costing. Direct traceability of costs becomes the key to improved decision making for pricing, product-line profitability analysis, make/buy decisions, and cost reduction. In addition, support costs should be traced to products through direct charging of activities.

CMS OBJECTIVES

The goal of a cost management system is to provide information to help companies use resources profitably to produce services or products that are competitive in terms of cost, quality, functionality, and timing in the world market. Within this context, a cost management system can be defined as a management planning and control system with the following objectives:

- To identify the cost of resources consumed in performing significant activities of the firm (accounting models and practices)
- To determine the efficiency and effectiveness of the activities performed (performance measurement)
- To identify and evaluate new activities that can improve the future performance of the firm (investment management)
- To accomplish the three previous objectives in an environment characterized by changing technology (manufacturing practices)

Goals of CMS

CMS will assist management in improving the traceability of costs. Many significant costs that could be attributed to products, processes, or projects are buried in overhead. These costs are then allocated based on arbitrary or inappropriate relations that distort product costs. Costs related to technology, tooling, work-in-process, maintenance, data processing, and engineering should be traced directly to those products and processes that consume them. In today's manufacturing, much information exists for improving the traceability of costs.

CMS will help companies optimize life-cycle performance. The total profitability of a product depends upon trade-offs made in the product life-cycle stages of engineering, manufacturing, and support. CMS will make visible the factors influencing total life-cycle performance. One important ramification of the life-cycle concept is to capitalize many costs that traditionally have been expensed.

CMS will enhance decision-making tools. The focus of most cost accounting systems has been on reporting historical performance. Today's highly automated environment has caused more costs to become fixed, and dynamic decision tools are critical for survival. CMS will recognize the impact of product design on product cost, capacity management, make/buy decisions in capital-intensive environments, retention or abandonment analysis, and the monitoring of strategic decisions.

CMS will expand the investment management process. It will evaluate advanced manufacturing technologies as a portfolio of interrelated projects rather than on a stand-alone basis. Further, the performance of investment projects will be monitored to provide ongoing control to ensure that benefits are achieved.

CMS will integrate performance measurement criteria with financial performance. Competitive strategies like quality, lead time, and flexibility are important bases on which companies compete. Measures of these strategies are normally stated in nonfinancial terms, but it is important to convert such nonfinancial measures to financial terms to ensure consistency. In addition, CMS will highlight non-value-added costs to facilitate their elimination.

CMS will support various levels of automation and diverse manufacturing philosophies. Within a single manufacturing plant a company may employ various levels of manufacturing sophistication. CMS will be flexible enough to provide meaningful data regardless of the unique implementation of the system. It will also employ data-sharing standards to facilitate a company's migration to computer-integrated manufacturing. CMS will support external financial reporting. It will employ database concepts to enable a company to capture data only once to support multiple reporting requirements. CMS will support internal controls. A paperless manufacturing facility will require the development of nontraditional approaches to internal controls.

CMS Data Architecture

Typically, companies are organized by departments. Departments, in turn, are defined by function, business unit, product line, or project. To control a company, managers need both financial and nonfinancial information. Organization cost information is obtained by accumulating cost data for all activities performed by that organizational unit.

Cost centers should be established for significant homogeneous groupings of cost within an organizational unit. Also, they should be defined at the level of defined individual responsibility. Significant activities should be defined for each cost center. Certain activities, such as data entry, will transcend cost centers. To understand and control the cost of activities that transcend individual cost centers, summarization (for those activities) is needed across the company. Activity information is obtained by accumulating and extracting data across all cost centers for the desired activity or group of activities.

Cost elements are the category of resources consumed by a company, such as direct technology, direct labor, direct material, and supplies. The major cost elements suggested by CMS are included in "Manufacturing Practices" (Chapter 3). Accounting transactions for cost elements will be captured once and summarized to satisfy multiple requirements.

The performance of activities should also be defined in nonfinancial terms. Nonfinancial information can include categories like time, quality defects, flexibility, and transaction.

Target performance should be expressed in terms of standards, so that actual performance can be illustrated as follows:

Department	Machining
Cost center	Sheet metal
Activity	Machine small parts
Measures	
Cost element	Direct technology
	Direct labor
	Direct material
	.
	.
	.
	Overhead
Nonfinancial	Lead time
	Quality defects

Life-cycle management requires data to be accumulated for specific products or a product family and processes across all the activities that occur during the product's life cycle. Often, startup costs are accumulated by defining an engineering or manufacturing project. The life-cycle concept uses inception-to-date information in addition to the period data required to satisfy external financial reporting requirements.

CMS PRINCIPLES

The CMS Conceptual Design is based on a set of guiding principles. While these principles will apply in any manufacturing environment, the importance attached to implementing them will vary, based on the unique requirements of the industry and the company's specific environment. These principles, in general, are compatible with the existing cost accounting framework. However, taken as a total system, they represent a significant departure from the objectives and focus of existing cost accounting theory and practices.

Cost Principles

The objective of a cost management system is to measure the cost of resources consumed in performing significant activities of the business. Reporting must be sufficient to satisfy internal and external requirements, such as making strategic business decisions, planning and controlling routine operations, and determining income and financial position. Several guiding principles have been identified to assist in improved cost management.

Identify costs of non-value-added activities to improve use of resources. The cost of non-value-added production and support activities should be identified to provide the visibility and basis for their reduction and elimination.

Recognize holding costs as a non-value-added activity traceable directly to a product. Holding assets represents an important non-value-added cost. These assets must be financed through internal cash or external debt and equity. The cost associated with holding assets has traditionally been buried in overhead or ignored on financial reports. This cost can be calculated as an imputed cost for management reporting purposes.

Significant costs should be directly traceable to management reporting objectives. The usefulness of cost information is directly related to the accurate traceability of the costs to management reporting objectives. The intent is to capture them directly to the projects, processes, and products that use them. Accurate direct traceability demands that *all* fixed and variable costs be assigned. Separating costs into fixed and variable components is not meaningful for routine decisions.

Separate cost centers should be established for each homogeneous group of activities consistent with organizational responsibility. All costs should be collected by significant activity and should be associated with a cost center. Cost centers should be defined at a level where all costs have a meaningful cause-and-effect relation.

Activity-based cost accumulation and reporting will improve cost traceability. Significant activities can be identified and separated by the organizational units that perform them. The same activity may be performed in several cost centers, but the activity transactions will be collected once for the individual cost center performing the work.

Separate bases for allocations should be developed to reflect causal relations between activity costs and management reporting objectives. Where direct assignment of costs is not possible or economical, cost pools should be established to accumulate homogeneous costs and allocate them to the desired management reporting objectives. The allocation should be based on sound rules that emphasize the most appropriate cause-and-effect relations. Implementation of this concept can result in the use of multiple allocation bases (i.e., bases other than direct labor) and will require the capability to change bases as the cause-and-effect relations change.

Costs should be consistent with the requirement to support life-cycle management. CMS should support life-cycle costing, which is the accumulation of costs for activities that occur over the entire life cycle of a product. This includes recurring production costs as well as one-time or nonrecurring ones that take place during the product-development and product logistics support phases of a product's life.

Technology costs should be assigned directly to products. Technology costs should become a cost element on the same level as direct labor and direct materials. The increasing importance and materiality of technology costs dictate that they should be assigned directly to products, processes, and projects using the technology. The usage can be measured by machine hours or throughput time rather than by traditional fixed-time depreciation methods.

Actual product cost should be measured against target cost to support elimination of waste. A company should measure the progress in meeting established target costs. This feedback is critical if a company expects to reduce cost over the period alloted to achieve the target cost.

Cost-effective approaches for internal control should be developed as a company automates. An appropriate system of internal controls is fundamental to any accounting system. As a company automates, migrating to paperless operation, the checks and balances needed for good management practices should evolve to reflect manufacturing changes.

Performance Measurement Principles

The objectives of performance measurement are: (1) to measure how well business activities are being performed in relation to specific goals and objectives developed in the strategic planning process; (2) to support elimination of waste. A company requires both financial and nonfinancial information to measure performance. The information must be consistent if it is to be meaningful. In other words, performance improvement (such as reduced lead times) should be understandable in financial terms. To reach the desired performance measurement objectives, the following principles have been identified.

Performance measures should establish congruence with a company's objectives. Performance measures should provide the link between the activities of the business and the strategic planning process. Measures should be consistent with stated business objectives and should consider both internal and external factors required to achieve these objectives. The axiom "You get what you measure" should be remembered. The performance measures established should be totally within the accountability of the person performing the activity. The measures should cover the span of responsibility of the activity and should not overlap the responsibilities of others.

The method of quantifying and the purpose of every performance measure should be communicated to the appropriate tiers within the company. Relations between individual goals and company goals should be explained. Results of all performance measures should be visible to as many people as possible to focus attention, to encourage understanding, and to improve performance.

Performance measures should be established for significant activities. Accounting is responsible for measuring the inputs (costs) required to perform an activity, while performance measurement is responsible for measuring the output (effectiveness) of that activity. All significant activities should have specific measures established for them; however, the same statistics or level of detail may not be required for each activity performed.

Performance measures should be established to improve visibility of cost drivers. Performance measures must recognize cost drivers as the cause of cost. Improved understanding and visibility of drivers will assist managers in obtaining the proper information to control cost.

Financial and nonfinancial activities should be included in the performance measurement system. Once the significant activities have been identified, the measures established for them should be few, quantifiable, and easy to understand. Measures should be defined and expressed in relevant units of measure. Many measurements are best expressed as physical terms (e.g., time, transactions); however, these measures should be capable of being converted to financial terms.

Investment Management Principles

The objective of investment management is to identify the optimal set of resources and activities that will help the business achieve its stated goals and objectives with the minimum amount of waste.

Several guiding principles of investment management have been identified.

Investment management should be viewed as more than the capital budgeting process. Investment management should be viewed as identifying, evaluating, and implementing new activities, or alternative approaches for performing existing activities, to improve the future performance of the firm. Consider the product/process development and maintenance function. In many cases, the cost associated with this function is viewed as a period expense that is controlled through the operating budget. However, the long-term impact that the function has on a firm's cost structure and operational performance suggests that it should be viewed as a capital investment rather than as an operating expense.

Investment management decisions should be consistent with company goals. The starting point of the investment management process should be the strategic plan. Investments in advanced manufacturing technology should be driven by specific requirements of the product forecast and the company's strategy for dealing with technological change.

Multiple criteria should be used to evaluate investment decisions. Cost and financial ratios, such as return-on-investment (ROI), represent only one aspect of an investment. Resulting improvements in quality, throughput, and flexibility can be of strategic importance. Thus, the various financial and nonfinancial criteria of the strategic plan should be considered when evaluating candidate projects.

Investments and attendant risks should be considered interrelated elements of an investment strategy. The benefits of many advanced manufacturing technologies accrue when several manufacturing activities are linked. The sum of the benefits of individual project benefits may _not_ be the same as a group of projects, because of dependencies and synergies that may exist among the projects. Each investment should be analyzed for technological and economic risk. Technological risk depends primarily on whether the technology is commercially available or must be developed. It is also influenced by the estimated life of the new technology and its compatibility with the existing technology in the facility. The economic risk represents the probability that the technology will achieve the projected economic results.

Activity data should be traceable to the specific investment opportunity. Once the technology is implemented, CMS should capture and report the performance of new or revised activities and monitor the actual results. Activity accounting will improve the traceability of the data needed for investment justification and benefit tracking.

Investment management decisions should support the reduction or elimination of non-value-added activities. The focus of investment management is to identify and evaluate new activities or alternative approaches for executing existing activities to improve the overall performance of the company. Candidate investment projects should be analyzed to determine their impact in eliminating waste during the periods established by the strategic plan.

Investment management decisions should support achieving target cost. Investment decisions should support achieving the overall target-cost objective established to obtain the desired market share for a product. Investment decisions should be consistent with the activity level cost and performance requirements set to achieve the desired overall target cost.

CHAPTER 2

CMS Trends and Issues

T his chapter explores the background, manufacturing trends, cost accounting issues, investment justification issues, and performance measurement problems that accompany the change from traditional manufacturing to computer-integrated manufacturing (CIM). The discussion focuses on trends, issues, and obstacles in the development of effective cost management systems.

Manufacturers worldwide find themselves at a crossroads. The explosion in technology is changing the basis of competition throughout the world. In order to compete effectively, companies must strive to manufacture sophisticated products at a low cost while maintaining high quality and providing outstanding customer service (short lead times). Yet they must be able to deal with short product life cycles and increasing international competition.

Most manufacturers' facilities are not structured to meet these demands, and the transition to automated manufacturing is often difficult. A particularly important but not well understood difficulty is the role played by today's cost accounting systems. Information is not being provided in a format to help management identify, prioritize, and solve problems. Manufacturing managers are being asked to make important decisions *in spite of* available cost accounting information, not *because* it is relevant.

BACKGROUND AND MANUFACTURING TRENDS

The factory of today is significantly different, both physically and functionally, from that of the past. This difference will become more acute as factories continue to automate. A summary of some of the most significant trends that are reshaping the manufacturing environment follows.

Changed Basis of Competition

Advanced manufacturing technologies, through capital decay, are changing the basis of competition in the marketplace. Companies are becoming increasingly aware of Wickham Skinner's message that a manufacturing facility can be either a competitive weapon or a corporate millstone. Significant improvements in product, process, and shop-floor capabilities can change the basis of competition and force other companies in an industry to improve performance or risk loss of market share.

The impact of automation on the basis of competition is most evident when one considers the following developments:

- Improvements in material science and microcomputers have resulted in products with capabilities not achievable without automation.
- Reduction in manufacturing costs will occur when an automated process is substituted for a less efficient, nonautomated process.
- Products with higher levels of quality are possible because of improvements in computer-aided engineering and the inherent consistency of automation.
- Higher levels of reliability and maintainability are resulting in lower field-support costs with better customer service.
- Product delivery lead times are decreasing with the implementation of just-in-time concepts, process rationalization, and automation projects.

Once in place, advanced manufacturing technologies can permanently change the basis of competition in an industry. Advanced technologies can impact either product or processes. Advances in product technology, resulting from expanded features or new materials can make companies unable to produce new products with their existing manufacturing facilities. As these products replace the current product line, firms who do not upgrade their manufacturing capabilities cannot compete in the marketplace. Advances in process technology enable companies to gain a competitive advantage through excellence in manufacturing. The impact of improved process technologies on market share must be measured relative to competition. Companies must remember that they do not possess a monopoly on advanced manufacturing technologies. Competitors who implement strategically important technologies can gain a competitive advantage through reduced cost, improved quality, faster throughput time, and better response to customers.

Most investment justification techniques assume a constant future market share. This assumption ignores capital decay—lost sales due to technologically obsolete products and processes. In these times of significant technological and management change, companies who stagnate face loss of market share. Capital decay exists at both the industry and the individual company levels.

The Technology Explosion

The rate of change in manufacturing and process technology is accelerating. The history of manufacturing shows a steady trend of substituting technology for human labor. Approximately 90 percent of all current knowledge in engineering and the physical sciences was generated during the last thirty years. This technology explosion is not expected to abate in the foreseeable future. "There will be more technological change in the next ten to twenty years than has happened in all history," predicts Bruce Merrifield, U.S. Assistant Secretary of Commerce. Manufacturers are faced with a constantly changing environment and a wide proliferation of technology alternatives, many of which are in varying degrees of "proof of concept." Management tools like cost accounting should assist the manufacturing manager in making difficult decisions in this dynamic environment. Today, most cost accounting systems are not providing the information necessary to manage the transition to a factory of the future.

Shorter Product Life Cycles

Product life cycles are getting shorter, and the rate of engineering change is increasing. The accelerating rate of change of technology is dramatically shortening the life cycles of products and manufacturing facilities. Technological breakthroughs are providing alternative processes that frequently promise superior performance for less cost. Major assets are often technologically obsolete long before their useful lives can be realized. New manufacturing equipment is often based on the use of computer technology. A review of computer technology reveals that significant productivity advances occur at very frequent intervals, generally every three years or less.

Figure 2.1
Reduced Product Life Cycles

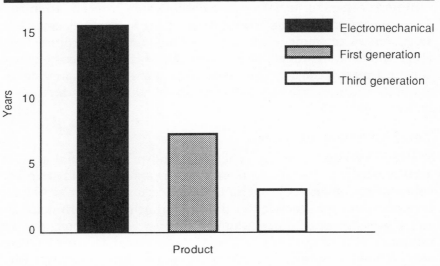

Source: Tony Isaac, The Plessey Company.

There is no reason to believe that this pattern will not continue in the future.

An example of this change was given by Tony Isaac, Director of Finance for Plessey Telecommunications and Office Systems Group. At the European CAM-I Cost Management Conference on March 25, 1986, Isaac indicated that "telecommunications is typical of an industry which has progressed at great speed from electromechanical equipment through electronics and two or three generations of digital technology in a short space of time." (See Figure 2.1.) With shorter product life cycles, there is an increasing need to understand the total product cost over its entire life cycle to determine profitability. Cost management systems should provide greater visibility of the impact of design considerations on manufacturing and support costs. Also, the impact of engineering changes on product/process cost should be understood in order to evaluate the need for engineering change.

Reduced product life has significant effects on manufacturing, such as less time available for firms to respond to changes in market demand and to recover product/process development costs; more engineering changes; and more new products and product variations necessary to satisfy market demands. This situation has increased the number of production options that must be considered in both long-range planning and daily operations. Firms that want to prosper in an advanced manufacturing environment must join technical/engineering competence with rigorous financial monitoring. A computerized life-cycle-oriented cost accounting system is required in this environment.

Better Production Flow

New manufacturing philosophies emphasize the need to keep inventory flowing through the factory. In the traditional environment inventory was used as a buffer against uncertainty (both demand and process), to maintain maximum resource utilization, and to minimize machine setups. These practices often resulted in long production cycle time, large amounts of work-in-process inventory, large amounts of floor space tied up, and significant production-control problems. Inventory obscured many production problems.

Improved Data Availability

Local Area Network (LAN) technology coupled with automated parts tracking and recognition technology are improving the availability and accuracy of data. In a manufacturing environment with long lead times between processes, an informal manual information system was sufficient. The introduction of advanced manufacturing technologies has increased dependence on computerized information. Manual data collection can seriously inhibit the effectiveness of an automated factory: often the data must be continually reviewed and corrected and so will not meet the timing requirements of an automated process. This problem is particularly vexing when companies reduce production cycle time as they automate, but fail to provide for timely information.

Although technology is the source of the problem it also provides the solution. The development of local area networks (LANs) and automated parts tracking/recognition technology will permit the various components of automation to be linked for control and communication. Anticipated advances in LAN technology over the next several years should decrease the cost and complexity and increase the reliability of this technology.

In spite of technological breakthroughs, much of the information captured in an automated environment is used primarily for local process decisions. Thus, while the availability and accuracy of data have improved, these data have not been integrated into the total manufacturing process.

Integrated Manufacturing Technologies

Advanced manufacturing technologies have traditionally been implemented as islands of technology. Future technologies will require an integrated approach, high capital investments, and long implementation cycles. In the traditional environment manufacturing processes could be incrementally replaced by newer, more efficient processes. Today, companies are attempting to develop integrated manufacturing systems comprising a harmonious flow of materials, tools, parts, and information through the factory. However, the difficulties of integration compound rapidly with the increased complexity of interconnecting the system components— physical connections, communication protocols, software, and data.

Companies are beginning to realize that automation alone will not guarantee the success of a manufacturing facility. Most manufacturing facilities are products of past unfocused manufacturing decisions. A company's strategic options can be limited by what appear to be routine manufacturing decisions, since these decisions can bind the company to facilities, equipment, and personnel that may take years to change.

Shift from Variable to Fixed Costs

Manufacturing factors of production are shifting from variable to fixed. Automation leads to a higher percentage of fixed cost because of its capital-intensity. Labor, on the other hand, is largely a variable cost, as reflected in the high rates of unemployment during recessionary times. Higher ratios of fixed costs (automation) to variable costs (labor) limit a company's ability to respond to changes in the economy. Traditional labor-intensive industries have been able to cut costs during a recession by laying off workers, a luxury not available when managing robots and flexible manufacturing systems.

COST ACCOUNTING ISSUES

As a result of changes in the manufacturing environment, several cost management issues have become more prominent.

Changing Cost-Behavior Patterns

As manufacturing facilities have become increasingly automated, cost-behavior patterns have changed. Overhead costs have risen dramatically and now exceed direct labor costs. Some of the more important changes include the following.

Smaller Direct-Labor Component. The cost-behavior patterns of manufacturing processes are shifting to a lower percentage of direct labor and a higher percentage of other, indirect costs. It is not uncommon to find that direct touch labor accounts for only 8–12 percent of total cost at many factories. This trend is predicted to be even more pronounced in the factory of the future.

Larger Equipment Component. A significant portion of total product cost is shifting to equipment-related costs. There has also been a decrease in the technological life of products and processes compared with their physical life.

Larger Information Component. With the introduction of advanced manufacturing technologies has come an increased dependence on computerized information. The impact of the information system on product cost is not widely understood in most manufacturing companies. Companies do not have a mechanism for evaluating the value added by more accurate information, data validation, maintenance, or the cost of poor decisions based on incorrect data. In addition, many of the information flows that were originally manual must be automated to increase their timeliness. Much of the information that was processed in batch mode must be processed in real-time.

Bases of Cost Allocation

Cost allocation is an inescapable problem: directly charging every expense to the lowest-level management reporting objective may not be possible and is seldom cost-effective. Given a specific management reporting objective and cost pool, managers must choose a basis of allocation that most accurately associates the expense with a specific management reporting objective. The process of allocation is characterized by a large number of computations and a misleading aura of precision.

Companies have always had to face the problem of choosing an appropriate cost-allocation technique. However, changing cost-behavior patterns demand that companies re-evaluate their allocation decisions continually. Many companies continue to cling to direct-labor-based allocations despite the reality of automation. As the relation between direct labor and the value added to a product by an automated manufacturing process becomes obscure, excessive burden rates develop. It is not uncommon to find burden rates that exceed 1000 percent. Further distortion can result when applying these rates to products on a labor-hours basis, since a single person may be responsible for multiple machines and may be working on several products simultaneously.

Changing the allocation basis alone, however, does *nothing* to change the trend from direct to indirect costs. Therefore, it is an illusion that changing the basis of allocation (for example, from direct labor to machine hours) will solve all cost management problems.

Improper Focus for Cost Reduction

Basing manufacturing decisions on a perceived, but invalid, relation between direct and indirect costs leads to poor manufacturing decisions. There have been cases of automation projects with documented savings in direct labor but with no corresponding reduction in total costs. Also, management usually focuses attention on those activities for which performance is reported. Studies by the United States Air Force (USAF) have shown that 75 percent of cost-reduction programs submitted by defense contractors focus on reducing direct touch labor rather than on making knowledge workers more productive or improving interfaces with suppliers. (See Figure 2.2.)

Figure 2.2
Cost-Reduction Focus

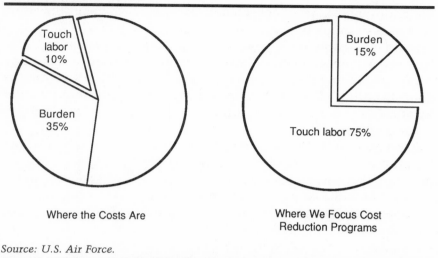

Where the Costs Are

Where We Focus Cost
Reduction Programs

Source: U.S. Air Force.

Changing Definitions of Cost

Definitions of cost classifications are shifting from indirect to direct. Manufacturers are faced with a larger pool of indirect costs and a smaller pool of direct costs. However, the determination of whether costs are direct or indirect is often a matter of definition and economics of data collection. Clearly, an environment with increasing indirect costs indicates that the definition of indirect costs must be reviewed.

In an advanced manufacturing environment the economies of data collection will be improved as companies implement LANs and automated parts-tracking systems. With the increased availability and accuracy of shop-floor data, many costs that were previously considered indirect can be evaluated and managed as direct costs, if appropriate.

Decreased Importance of Inventory Valuation

Inventory valuation is de-emphasized in an automated environment. Traditionally, the most important objective of the cost accounting process has been inventory valuation. High levels of work-in-process inventories, the result of traditional manufacturing philosophies, have focused much of the cost accounting effort on stage-of-completion valuation to accurately cost WIP.

Standard costing often aggravates the inventory-valuation problem. All variances must be forced out in the current accounting period by valuing the inventory at standard cost. This valuation is done by multiplying both the beginning and ending inventory units by standard costs and accounting for the change in the monthly income statement.

In an automated environment WIP inventory should be reduced to minimal levels, thereby simplifying the inventory-valuation problem. Work-in-process inventory should be small enough to permit easy determination of quantities and thus verification of inventory accuracy. The problem can be simplified further by using standard containers to facilitate physical counts and to allow easy identification of problem areas where WIP has increased. Also, the number of transactions decrease as the number of storerooms and WIP units decline. The need for obsolescence and inventory adjustment reserves also dwindles.

Obscured WIP Carrying Costs

Work-in-process represents the investment in goods in the process of being manufactured. Traditionally, WIP has been defined to comprise direct materials, direct labor, and a portion of factory overhead. This cost is accumulated as a current asset on the balance sheet and is used for computing the cost of goods manufactured, a prime determinant of product profitability.

This cost-accumulation approach does not segregate related costs that are incurred along with WIP, such as finance cost, obsolescence and scrap, material storage, material movement, taxes, insurance, WIP inventory accounting, and production control inefficiencies to cope with high WIP. Each of these costs is caused by WIP but are captured in individual cost categories not directly associated with WIP. These costs are called carrying charges. As manufacturing throughput is reduced, the costs associated with carrying the inventory are reduced proportionally.

Changing Bases of Calculating Depreciation

Current depreciation methods assume that technology wears out over time and that its cost should be recovered over a fixed period. Current depreciation methods are based on fixed-time recovery of the cost of plant and equipment. Fixed-time depreciation assumes uniform usage throughout the asset life. These methods assume that value added to the product is independent of individual products and actual utilization during the recovery period.

The current practice of charging depreciation expense to overhead and then allocating the cost to products can result in significant cost distortion. Products that are technology-intensive often do not absorb a fair share of the overhead, resulting in a product cost distortion. To illustrate, we have identified two products with equal production volume. Product A is technology-intensive, and product B is labor-intensive. With a value-added approach for depreciation, the true cost of both products would be the same—$925. (See Table 2.1.) The overhead rate, based on labor dollars, would be computed as

$$\text{Overhead} = \frac{\text{Total cost } - \text{ Direct labor and material}}{\text{Total direct-labor cost}}$$

$$= \frac{\$1,000}{\$250} = 400\%$$

The traditional cost accounting approach would apply the overhead to the direct-labor hours using the 400 percent overhead rate. With this approach, the product cost for A would be $550 and for B would be $1,300, a 40 percent error. (See Table 2.2.) The reason for this distortion is that the overhead rate is inflated by the technology cost. The inflated overhead cost is then allocated to the

Table 2.1

	PRODUCT A	PRODUCT B
Direct labor	$ 50	$200
Direct material	300	300
Direct technology	200	50
Other overhead	375	375
Total product cost	$925	$925

Table 2.2

	PRODUCT A	PRODUCT B
Direct labor	$ 50	$ 200
Direct material	300	300
Overhead	200 ($50 × 400%)	800 ($200 × 400%)
Total product cost	$550	$1,300

products using an erroneous direct-labor basis. In fact, the relation between labor and technology is diametric rather than complementary. This example illustrates the potentially misleading management information that can result from inappropriate depreciation.

An alternative that is in accordance with Generally Accepted Accounting Practices (GAAP), but not widely used, is to depreciate equipment cost based on machine hours rather than on fixed periods. It offers the advantage of a better match of automation expense to those products (and only those products) that use the technology. Another advantage of the method is that changing economic conditions would result in lessening the impact of economic cycles. Another approach might be to allocate costs on inventory velocity (the WIP time for a part) to encourage companies to reduce factory throughput time.

The depreciation process is also complicated by the need to determine the basis of depreciation. Companies need insight into the technological value, as well as the book value, of capital equipment. One step in this direction would be to use the technological life for depreciation calculations. Sound accounting requires equipment life to be based on the shorter of tax, technological, or physical life. However, most companies use tax-allowable life even though it may be unrealistic.

It is common practice today to depreciate manufacturing equipment over its useful life of eight, ten, or even twelve years. Also, shorter technological lives will force a company to recover the cost of automation in shorter periods, or to make the manufacturing process more responsive to changing requirements.

Current methods of accounting for technology have distorted technology costs and have often prevented companies from investing in badly needed technologies because of the resulting write-off situation. If the owner has elected to depreciate the cost over a traditional useful life and to finance the equipment over a long term, a severe financial penalty will occur if the company decides to replace the equipment. Chances are this penalty was not considered when evaluating product costs and related pricing decisions, because traditional accounting methods treat gain or loss on disposition of property and financing costs as below-the-line costs rather than a part of product cost.

Timeliness of Information

As companies migrate to a CIM environment, the need for real-time data must be weighed against the increased cost of the information. Failure to upgrade the cost management system to support the automated process will degrade the efficiency of the entire automated process.

Inadequacy of Period Reporting

Period reporting hinders management decisions. Shorter product life cycles result in less latitude for management error, since the cost-recovery periods are short. Today's cost accounting systems are based on period reporting and do not provide life-cycle reporting. This hinders management's understanding of product-line profitability and the potential cost impact of long-term decisions about engineering design changes.

The primary determinants of life-cycle costs occur during the engineering design phase (see Figure 2.3).

Providing Financial Data to Design and Process Engineers

Many choices and trade-offs occur in product and process development. These are a function of product performance requirements, physical properties of the materials involved, and manufacturing capabilities and limitations of the facility. The product specifications usually lock in the majority of the material cost, because the performance characteristics and product cost goals are normally specified. Also, the range of manufacturing processes primarily depends on the materials selected. Thus, design and process decisions

Figure 2.3
Life-Cycle Costs

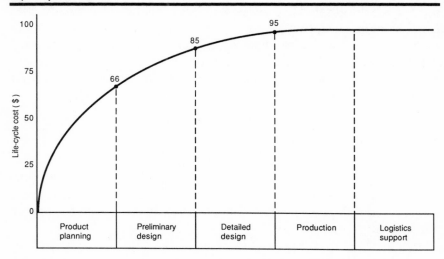

Source: *Adapted from Benjamin S. Blanchard,* Design and Manage to Life-Cycle
Cost. *Portland, OR: M/A Press, 1978.*

can have a long-term impact on a company's cost structure. Shorter
product life cycles have resulted in less latitude for management
error, since the cost-recovery period also decreases.

At present, development costs, which can represent a sizable
investment of capital whose benefits accrue over many years, are
not directly identified with the product being developed. They are,
instead, treated as a period expense, buried in overhead, and allocated to all products (typically as direct labor). Many companies
use life-cycle models for planning and budgeting new products. But
they fail to integrate these models with existing cost accounting
systems to provide feedback on planning effectiveness and on how
design decisions affect operational and support costs (even years
later). Cost accounting systems have focused primarily on the cost
of physically producing the product, without accumulating costs
over the entire design, manufacture, market, and support cycle.
Life-cycle costing and reporting would provide management with a
better picture of product profitability and would help managers
gauge the effectiveness of their planning activities.

Figure 2.4
Product Life Cycle

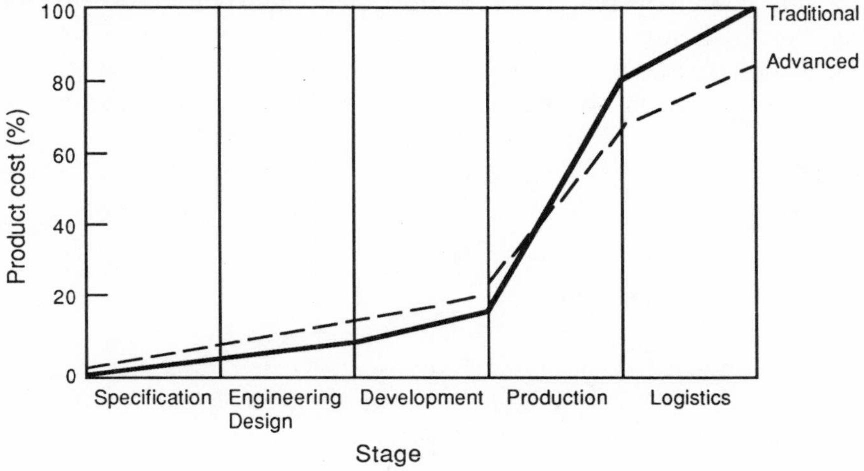

Source: United Technologies Corporation.

Expanding Emphasis on Process Engineering

Traditionally, only about 5 percent of the product life-cycle costs have been allocated to the conceptual and validation planning phases. Instead, companies have focused engineering design on product features, leaving many of the decisions on equipment configuration, operational planning, and organizational issues to be made on an ad hoc basis by manufacturing and operating personnel. Today, many foreign competitors are spending considerably more money and time in planning activities. This has often resulted in lower production costs, reduced time from design to manufacture, higher quality, greater flexibility, and lower product life-cycle costs. The relations of costs over the product cycle are illustrated in Figure 2.4. In the future, a greater percentage of product cost will be allocated to the engineering phase.

Inflated Burden Rates Distort Product Cost

Today, product cost information is distorted by burden rates that have become, in many companies, so high as to be almost unmanageable. The problem is compounded when companies cling to a direct-labor allocation method despite the fact that overhead costs are not related to direct labor. Invalid product cost allocation is occurring when indirect costs far exceed direct costs (typically, direct labor or machine hours), or when the relation between the basis of allocation and the indirect costs has become obscure. A primary reason for this distortion is that the overhead rate is inflated by technology costs. The inflated overhead cost is then allocated to the products using an erroneous direct-labor basis.

Controlling Overhead

Current product cost reporting buries nonproductive costs in overhead. Overhead has increased dramatically. Current approaches for capturing overhead costs and allocating them to products disguises a series of complex factors that affect a firm's cost structure. The calculation and aggregate reporting of overhead by traditional cost accounting systems has hindered management's understanding of what comprises overhead costs and of the cost implications of nonproductive activities. Product-cost reports should assist managers in identifying opportunities to eliminate waste. They should include such costs as WIP inventory carrying costs, quality, engineering changes, production/schedule changes, estimating inaccuracies, increased support activities, and unforeseen problems.

Functional Orientation

Today, many managers associate work responsibility with organizational structure. While this approach is consistent with organizational objectives as expressed in financial budgets, there is no assurance that the organization of cost centers is consistent with manufacturing functions. This has made it increasingly difficult to budget and report performance at the responsibility level. Ideally, cost center structure should mirror the manufacturing processes that exist in the facility. All too often the cost accounting system has no relation to actual operations on the shop floor.

Promoting Companywide Efficiency

Management practices often focus on improving departmental rather than companywide efficiency by reducing direct costs. The most common form of management organization in the United States and Europe is a divisional structure. Under divisional management, companies organize by function: finance, design engineering, marketing, manufacturing process. Managers are given responsibility for their functional areas and are held accountable for the efficiency of their departments. In this environment they will focus on projects that will improve efficiency in their departments by reducing direct costs such as labor and operating expenses. There is no incentive to reduce costs that do not impact their own areas of responsibility. This is suboptimal management for the company as a whole.

Revising Cost Center Structure

In a traditional manufacturing environment, where machine tools are relatively simple, manually operated (one person, one machine), and of similar value, the entire shop floor is often treated as a single cost center. This approach is very simple and gives reasonably accurate results. In an automated environment, however, there are a wide variety of machine tools, which require minimal human support and which are complex and expensive production systems. Too often, in this new environment, companies simply adjust the overhead rate to include the increased value of the new machinery rather than creating new cost centers. Each product thus bears a proportion of the cost of the new equipment, even though it may not be processed by that equipment, and products that are technology-intensive often do not absorb a fair share of the overhead.

However, managers must also keep in mind that excess cost centers increase cost accounting complexity and reporting costs. Cost accounting systems add costs to a product without adding corresponding value. These cost increases must be offset against the costs associated with making bad decisions.

IMPACT OF AUTOMATED ENVIRONMENTS ON INTERNAL CONTROL PROCEDURES

The integration of automated processes through LANs will result in fewer physical documents. This paperless environment will have a significant impact on internal control procedures and accountability.

Desirability of Standard Information Systems Interfaces

Today, management information software designed by one vendor is often incompatible with that of other vendors. The solution to this growing "Tower of Babel" is a standard interface for cost management information and automated equipment.

Assigning Capacity-Related Costs to Products

As fixed costs increase, the impact of capacity-related costs must be identified and assigned to specific products. Capacity decisions have a long-term impact on a firm's cost structure and pricing strategy. Products should be charged for the resources consumed in manufacturing, and any excess or future capacity costs associated with specific product lines must be understood. Ultimately, prices must recover full costs (plus an adequate return on the capital invested). Current approaches mask the impact of capacity-related costs, distort product profitability, and make pricing decisions more difficult.

INVESTMENT JUSTIFICATION ISSUES

Many companies currently struggle with cost justification and tracking the benefits of advanced manufacturing technologies. Organizations often adhere strictly to tough ranking methods, by which likely costs are matched against the contribution the project is likely to yield. These methods often use data that are outside the current cost accounting systems. Benefits are elusive and cost estimates often unrealistic. The problems of investment justification as applied today lie not in the concept of rigorous financial analysis as much as in the fact that the information is usually tactical rather than strategic. Cost management systems traditionally have not supplied this information.

When evaluating investments in radically new manufacturing methods that require relatively large expenditures, managers face several practical obstacles.

Poorly Understood Cost-Behavior Patterns

The cost-behavior patterns of new technologies are rarely well understood. Traditional justification methodologies focus on easily quantifiable costs such as direct labor and direct material. However, manufacturing excellence goes beyond these traditional measures and includes quality, flexibility, throughput time, and responsiveness to customers. Excluding these important factors penalizes investments in advanced manufacturing technologies.

Excessively High Hurdle Rates

Organizations often adhere to ranking methods where likely costs are matched against the forecasted contributions of projects. Projects then are selected only when they are judged likely to exceed the established hurdle rate. It is a common mistake to believe that high discount rates will ensure that only high-return projects will be selected. This approach penalizes long-term investments, because the compounding effect of high discounted cash flow (DCF) rates causes future benefits to be discounted heavily. Similarly, management schemes that insist on short payback periods exclude many advanced technology projects.

Lack of Portfolio Approach

Project investment opportunities are typically analyzed on an individual basis rather than as part of an investment portfolio. An optimized manufacturing facility cannot be bought as a turn-key product. Many of the necessary technologies have not been developed; others may be commercially available to varying degrees. Finally, the selection of projects will depend on an individual company's current manufacturing capabilities, competition in its industry, and company-specific cost drivers.

In this environment it is easier to undertake a series of small incremental, independent improvements than to make global changes. Typically, capital-investment budgets of most organizations consist of a collection of small projects whose objectives are to replace existing equipment with more productive alternatives, to increase capacity, or to alleviate bottlenecks. These projects normally are easy to justify through direct-labor savings.

In contrast, the benefits of many advanced manufacturing technologies accrue when several manufacturing activities are linked. The sum of the benefits of the individual projects will *not* be equal to total savings. Evaluation of individual projects will result in both double-counting and overlooking synergistic benefits that occur when several projects are implemented. For example, a company may evaluate a sophisticated solid-modeling system and a generative process-planning system. If analyzed individually, the synergistic effects of these related projects might be missed. Similarly, several projects—for example, just-in-time (JIT) manufacturing, flexible manufacturing systems (FMS), and computer-aided process planning (CAPP) systems—may independently reduce a cost element (such as inventory), but productivity improvement will occur primarily when the first technology is implemented and will be affected less in subsequent implementations of related technologies. Creating a portfolio involves developing a time-phased plan in which project costs and benefits are linked over a period of five to ten years.

Limitations on Future Technology Decisions

Previous technology decisions often bind or impact future technology decisions. As companies automate, their risk positions change as the cost-behavior patterns shift from variable to fixed. Past technology selection often becomes an important inhibitor of future market flexibility. Companies that commit significant capital investment to specialized equipment for specific products or product families may be limiting their strategic options. Decisions to retire technologies for which the cost has not been recovered fully are very difficult and usually are viewed negatively by the external capital markets.

Inadequate Cost-Benefit Information

Information needed for cost-benefit analysis is often not available, nor is there adequate ongoing monitoring. Traditional accounting systems use absorption costing to determine product cost. Most investment justification methodologies use variable or marginal costing principles. This creates conflict with the cost accounting system, since only those costs directly affected by the new technology are included in the justification process.

Also, most investment-justification methodologies often use data considered "unquantifiable" and outside the scope of traditional cost accounting systems. The result is that benefits have been elusive and cost estimates often have been unrealistic. Historically, management most willingly accepts those decision-making criteria that can be easily quantified.

Good management practice dictates that a company should monitor those activities that can help manage the business. Accounting systems should be linked to control those planned activities and should provide control information based on established accounting principles.

PERFORMANCE MEASUREMENT ISSUES

Most cost accounting systems are historical, oriented toward financial reporting, and inadequate to measure operational performance. The strategic benefits of automation accrue not only to lower cost but also to improved quality, shorter production cycles, and a greater responsiveness to changing requirements. For example, improved quality opens new markets that demand higher-precision products and gives the manufacturer an edge when competing for old markets.

Traditionally, operational performance measures have been used as an indication of manufacturing operation effectiveness. However, performance measurements typically do not attain the same visibility as financial information, either internally or externally. The cost management accounting system should ensure that general goals, such as enhanced flexibility, are reported with explicit operational meanings.

Traditional performance measurement systems ignore inventory levels in assessing the effectiveness of the production process. They focus on machine utilization and report direct labor by operation, and they frequently include rework/replacement effort as part of earned value when measuring productivity (that is, they exclude quality as a factor in performance measurement). Current systems measure individual work-center productivity rather than tying measurement and rewards to the productivity of the shop, assembly line, or plant of which they are a part.

The Importance of Monitoring Strategic Projects

New cost management systems must be able to monitor strategic projects. Traditional cost accounting systems have focused primarily on the cost of physically producing the product (conversion costs). This provides a special mechanism for monitoring and controlling significant long-term investments that could be vital for a company's survival.

Examples of strategic projects could be multiyear programs to develop new technologies, to improve quality, or to train workers. These types of projects may often be stated as qualitative goals or objectives. However, they might affect many people and activities within the facility. As with any major expenditure or project, costs need to be collected, to be compared to budgets, and to be reported over long periods. This implies that the cost management system needs a project-reporting capability. There could be significant overlap with other engineering and manufacturing activities, but costs may not be identifiable with a specific product or contract at that time. Different levels of cost detail must be accommodated. The cost management system must be able to report the information regularly and to handle different accounting treatments (expense versus capitalization) of the *individual* cost elements.

The Importance of Identifying Cost Drivers

Most cost accounting systems are oriented toward work orders and do not identify adequately the impact of cost drivers on the cost of individual manufacturing processes. Today, the direct-labor orientation of most manufacturing managers results in the attitude that responsibility and organizational structure are one and the same. However, many costs incurred in one department are caused by decisions made in other departments.

Many strategic planners believe that the best way to control costs is to monitor and control cost drivers. Examples of cost drivers, as developed by Arthur Andersen & Co. in the Accounting Futures Study, include engineering change orders, space utilization, forecast errors, master scheduling changes, inventory levels, product design and lack of interchangeable components, and multiple bills of material.

WHY THE SLOW PACE?

One reason leading-edge manufacturers are growing impatient for solutions to cost management problems is that, until now, the development of a cost management knowledge base has been handled largely on an ad hoc basis. Individual companies have recognized the problem. Many have attempted to solve the problem internally. But despite these well-intentioned efforts, changes in CMS practices are occurring at an unacceptably slow pace. Research for the CAM-I CMS Conceptual Design points out several reasons for the slow advance toward modern, fully integrated CMS schemes.

Insufficient Knowledge Base

There is no well-developed base of knowledge. The opinions of CMS experts range from those who advocate slow, evolutionary change (believing existing knowledge is sufficient) to those who advocate revolutionary change to discover and develop the necessary knowledge.

In either case, there is no standard definition for *cost management*. To some, it means cost accounting and the determination of product cost. To others, it means the measurement of nonfinancial, operational factors of production. Still others say it is management accounting and therefore totally separate from external reporting requirements. However, most people will agree that it is an area of management that, in its current state, is inadequate to support today's factory operations.

Limits of Practicality

Many well-intentioned efforts to upgrade accounting systems often fail when they achieve a level of sophistication that cannot be achieved uniformly throughout a manufacturing facility. Most manufacturing environments are a mix of automated and manual processes. Any effort to develop a uniform information system must be able to operate within this spectrum.

External Factors

Financial information requirements are highly regulated. External organizations such as the Securities and Exchange Commission, the Internal Revenue Service, the Department of Defense, and public accounting firms exert significant influence on cost accounting practices. Given this environment of external regulation, reforming the framework of generally acccepted cost accounting practices is beyond the capabilities of any individual company.

Conservative Bias

The users of financial information require objective, consistent information. Financial information has been getting "softer" (i.e., lower direct costs) in the age of automation. Many companies cling to direct labor-based reporting because they can "touch and feel" it more easily than such concepts as quality and flexibility.

Manufacturing Complexity

Manufacturing processes have been shifting slowly from a manual environment, where the goal of automation was to increase worker productivity, to a CIM environment, where automation controls the pace of manufacturing. With this changing environment has come an increase in the complexity of manufacturing processes and a concomitant difficulty in understanding the financial and operational cost drivers.

CHAPTER 3

Manufacturing Practices

T his chapter describes the various manufacturing environments in which CMS will operate during the next ten to fifteen years. It provides a common set of assumptions for the CMS design; a baseline for understanding the implications of advanced manufacturing technologies and manufacturing strategies for the activities of a firm; suggestions for identifying and eliminating waste; and a basis for predicting information requirements for the CMS.

The first three sections present a conceptual model of a generic discrete parts manufacturer. The model is applicable in any environment and supports the elimination of waste. The last section discusses quality management, which is viewed as a prerequisite to company success in today's competitive environment.

ENGINEERING/MANUFACTURING OBJECTIVES

This section describes a set of generic objectives that represent an ideal facility where there is no waste. The objectives are not intended to represent radically new concepts but rather to portray the current views of manufacturing strategies. These views are dynamic; they would have been expressed much differently, and would have received different emphasis, five or ten years ago. Recent advances in product and process technology, new manufacturing strategies such as Just-in-Time and Total Quality Control (TQC), and the impact of international competition have resulted in these changed views. The manufacturing objectives are stated in *absolute* terms (for example, *zero* defects instead of *minimum* defects) to emphasize the need for changing corporate mind-set to one of continual pursuit of improvement. A company can restructure its activities to accomplish one or more of the objectives. Furthermore, progress toward the objectives can be measured using CMS techniques.

The goal of any manufacturing entity is to structure its activities to utilize resources efficiently to produce products that are competitive in terms of cost, quality, function, and timing (in the world market). A company can realize this goal by applying advanced manufacturing technologies and management strategies like JIT/ TQC and CIM to eliminate wasteful (non-value-added) activities. Optimized manufacturing is the optimal use of all pertinent tools and techniques to accomplish business goals without waste.

In the past, it was common practice to work toward economically balanced levels of inventory, quality, and other critical factors of production. Training programs focused on instilling a cost-benefit mentality in manufacturing managers. The Economic Order Quantity (EOQ) concept is a classic example of such training.

The cost-benefit concept was applied to all aspects of manufacturing. For example, if a product line had an annual production level of $3 million, we might view the impact of reducing scrap as follows.

	SCRAP REDUCTION	
SCRAP RATE	POTENTIAL SAVINGS	ACTION
2.0%	$60,000	Yes
1.0	30,000	Marginal
0.5	15,000	No

This fits the concept of diminishing returns—the lower the level of value returned, the less economically attractive it is to expend a high level of effort. Thus, managers schooled in cost-benefit thinking would drive the scrap rate down to around 1 percent and thereafter consider the resulting dollar loss economically acceptable. Today, however, strong competition from quality-minded foreign producers forces manufacturers to work toward absolute quality and to realize that quality and cost are complementary—raising quality decreases cost. Competitors are using this concept very successfully to capture market share.

The CMS Conceptual Design identifies ten generic engineering/ manufacturing objectives that provide a basis for optimized manufacturing. A company can restructure its activities to accomplish one or more of these objectives and can measure its progress using the CMS techniques. Each company will place different emphasis on achieving its individual mix of manufacturing objectives; it will establish priorities based on its industry, its products, the competitive strategies it adopts, and its markets.

1. Produce for Demand

Every piece should be produced according to demand. It is advantageous to trigger production by actual rather than forecast demand, avoiding inventory buildup. Large finished-goods inventories lead to large holding costs and potential obsolescence costs. Such expenses are non-value-added. They can be eliminated by shortening manufacturing lead time through increased flexibility, electronic links, and improved vendor relations.

DRIVERS
Accurate forecasts/customer demand
Manufacturing capability
Capacity constraints
Production cycle time
Manufacturing philosophies/policies
System responsiveness

2. Detect the Best Product Design

Of the many alternative product designs, one exists that meets specifications, is the least costly to produce, is perceived as having a high degree of quality, is easy to maintain, and is highly reliable within tolerances defined by the product specifications. The shaded area in Figure 3.1 illustrates the difference in costs (non-value-added) between the actual and the optimal life-cycle costs.

DRIVERS
Manufacturing capabilities/constraints
Material technology (substitutions)
Make/buy policy
Vendor capabilities/material availability
Quality specifications
Marketing specifications

Figure 3.1
Actual and Optimal Life-Cycle Costs

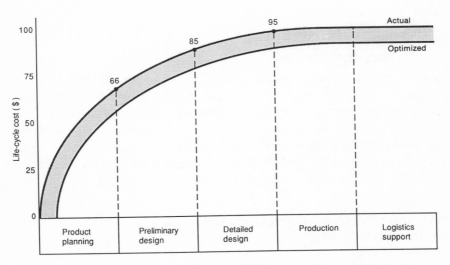

Source: Adapted from Benjamin S. Blanchard, Design and Manage to Life-Cycle Cost. *Portland, OR: M/A Press, 1978.*

3. Minimize Product Delivery Time

It is beneficial to design, build, and deliver a product to the customer in the shortest possible time, without sacrificing the goals of low cost, high quality, ease of maintenance, and reliability. There are three important dimensions in the product delivery cycle: (1) engineering design and development; (2) production; (3) customer delivery.

Engineering Design and Development. This part of the product delivery cycle includes the time from product specification until the release of the product design to manufacturing. The primary advanced manufacturing technologies that affect delivery times during this part of a product's life cycle are Group Technology (GT), feature technology, computer-aided design, computer-aided engineering (simulation), computer-aided testing (structural analysis, simulation), computer-aided process planning (generative, variant), automated bills of material, numerical control (NC) program generation, life-cycle analysis, design-to-cost methodologies, and artificial intelligence/expert systems.

DRIVERS
Customer requirements
Degree of parts standardization
Integration of activities in the engineering cycle
Knowledge gap (automated versus manual methods)
Product complexity
Design standards
Make/buy policy

Production. This part of the product delivery cycle includes the manufacturing cycle time. Manufacturing cycle time is composed of process time, inspection time, move time, and wait time. In the optimized manufacturing environment, inspection time, move time, and wait time will be eliminated. The primary advanced manufacturing technologies that affect delivery times during this part of a product's life cycle are automated manufacturing equipment (robots, NC, CNC, DNC, and other specialized equipment); flexible manufacturing systems (FMS); and manufacturing planning and control systems (order entry, capacity planning, master production scheduling and forecasting, Material-Requirements Planning [MRP], inventory management, factory scheduling, shop-floor control).

DRIVERS
Manufacturing philosophy (machine utilization, buffers)
Knowledge (cross-training/worker flexibility, learning curves)
Plant layout
Bottlenecks/imbalances
Demand stability (degree of forecast stability)
Diversity of product mix
Performance measures
Design standardization
New product introductions
Process plan/sequence dependencies

Scrap/yield/rework
Engineering change notices (ECNs)
Documentation accuracy (inventory, routings, billing, standards)
Setups
Supplier relation/on-schedule performance

Customer Delivery. This part of the product delivery cycle includes both the time from the shipping dock to the customer site, and the customer acceptance cycle. While the former is normally beyond the reach of advanced manufacturing technologies, the customer acceptance cycle is directly affected by automated order entry and dispatching systems.

There is a direct correlation between time and profitability. By shortening engineering design and development time, companies can introduce products more quickly than their competitors and thus increase market share. Long design-cycle times also result in higher engineering costs, since more resources (staffing and overhead) are used to produce identical output. As the length of the design time increases, initial market share projections may be invalidated by changes in technology that render a design obsolete or by the introduction of similar products by competitors.

Production time also has a significant cost impact. Companies must finance work-in-process inventory during production. Longer lead times require more sophisticated production-control procedures. Other costs, such as facilities for storage of inventory, material handling, and WIP inventory accounting must also be absorbed in product cost. These are non-value-added costs, which could be minimized by reducing cycle time.

4. Strive for Zero Defects

Quality influences profitability. "Building it right the first time" eliminates many costs associated with poor quality, such as rework, scrap, warranty, inventory levels, inspection requirements, and information systems. All such costs are considered non-value-added, since they could be eliminated by achieving perfect quality. This objective requires an attitude of continual improvement and a high degree of worker involvement.

DRIVERS
Product specifications (tolerances)
Process capabilities and limitations
Procurement quality
Product producibility
Knowledge
Manufacturing philosophies
Human error and variability
Breakdown/wear
Setups
Engineering change notices
Tooling
Schedule stability
Inspection points and time

5. Use Optimal Means of Production

The optimal combination of technology, people, and material should be used for each manufacturing process. This does not necessarily imply that automation is the ultimate solution. For certain operations, direct labor may be the optimal means of production. However, a manufacturer should be able to discern the optimal means of production for each process and to apply it dynamically. Furthermore, the manufacturer must be able to identify, measure, and apply the factors of production necessitated by employing the optimal means.

For each operation, there is a method of manufacturing that would result in the maximum performance and the lowest life-cycle cost. The difference between the ideal method and the actual method employed represents non-value-added costs. The optimal method changes as production technology and costs change with time.

DRIVERS
Resource limitations (capital; trained labor pool; material sources)
Knowledge
Product variability, volumes, and useful life cycle
Product specification (material; complexity/performance requirements)

Forecast accuracy
Documentation accuracy (routings, billing, standards)
Engineering change notices
Producibility

6. Strive for Zero Time between Manufacturing Operations

Non-value-added costs accrue when inventory is idle. Studies show that WIP inventory is idle more than 90 percent of the time. Non-value-added costs such as WIP carrying costs, material handling, and associated overhead costs can be reduced greatly by minimizing move time, queue time, and in-process stores. As the time between manufacturing operations approaches zero, manufacturing flow improves.

DRIVERS
Lot sizes
Setup time
Availability of factors of production (machine, tooling, labor, materials)
Product volume/product diversity/commonality of parts
Routing complexity/process planning
Plant layout/multisite manufacturing
Material handling
Information availability
Information accuracy
Schedule changes
Knowledge
Vendor reliability
Policies

7. Strive for Zero Setup Time

Setup time is non-value-added because it causes idle inventories and increases production time. Lengthy setups also require large lot sizes to reduce the effect of time lost. If on-line setup time is reduced, it becomes economical to produce in small lots. Small lots facilitate better quality, early defect detection, lower WIP, and reduced overhead costs. Setup time is often treated as a fixed production factor. However, it can be reduced dramatically by using specially engineered tools and machines, tool cartridges, and setup synchronization (parallel setup, tooling proximity).

DRIVERS (ZERO SETUP TIME)
Small-lot processing
Workplace layout/proximity of tools

DRIVERS (ACTUAL/STANDARD SETUP TIME)
Knowledge (operator training)
Availability of factors of production (machine, tooling, labor, materials)
Machine configuration
Tool design
Product variability/parts standardization
Production sequence (similar parts)
Policies (worker flexibility; standards—not having allowance)
Schedule changes
Information availability
Information accuracy

DRIVERS (MINIMUM PROCESS TIME)
Product design (complexity; tolerance requirements; physical properties of materials; shape/size of raw material)
Product producibility
Product volume/product diversity/commonality of parts
Process capabilities and limitations
Knowledge
Information availability
Information accuracy
Material quality
Policies (worker flexibility)
Workplace layout
Process routing

8. Maintain Zero Raw-Material and Finished-Goods Inventories

Maintaining inventories is non-value-added because of the high costs associated with carrying inventory, including interest, facilities, obsolescence, insurance, and taxes. Ideally, purchased items should reach the factory just in time to be used in the production process. If goods can be produced according to demand, there is no need to carry finished goods as a buffer against production lead times.

DRIVERS (ZERO RAW-MATERIAL INVENTORY)
Supplier management (number of vendors, alternative vendors; vendor location/transportation; frequent deliveries; raw-material lead time; vendor capacity; material scarcity; communication/ scheduling; purchasing/vendor policies)
Forecast accuracy
Generic versus proprietary components
Policies
Standardization of components
Make/buy decisions
Knowledge
Information availability
Information accuracy
In-process stock points

DRIVERS (ZERO FINISHED-GOODS INVENTORY)
Stocking policy
Forecast accuracy
Customer relations (proximity of location; frequency of delivery)
Knowledge
Distribution system
Product obsolescence
Information availability
Information accuracy

9. Minimize Management and Support Structures

It is to a company's benefit to achieve all manufacturing objectives with a minimum of management activity. Most organizational structures were developed more than twenty or thirty years ago and are characterized by too many layers of management, too much red tape and paperwork, and too many people (support staff too large). These costs can be reduced significantly by simplifying procedures, streamlining the organization, and minimizing management activities.

DRIVERS
Organizational layers
Transactions

Management policies (degree of autonomy in decision making; distributed versus centralized control)
Forecast accuracy and stability
External factors/compliance
Knowledge
Information availability
Information accuracy

10. Minimize Total Life-Cycle Costs

The difference between the lowest possible life-cycle cost for a product and its actual cost represents non-value-added costs, which can be eliminated. Because product life cycles are becoming shorter, it is even more important to understand how life-cycle cost relates to profitability. Minimizing product costs during a particular reporting period does not always result in reduced total life-cycle cost. A long-term perspective is required for accurate product cost reporting. Product cost reports should now include life-cycle-to-date data in addition to accounting-period related figures. Cost distributions will change as more costs occur upstream (in the design and planning phases) to ensure downstream savings. Also, the focus of engineering must include both an emphasis on product-related features and planning for manufacturability.

DRIVERS
Knowledge
Performance measures
Process capabilities and limitations
Management philosophy
Information availability
Information accuracy
Product variability, volumes, and useful life cycle
Product delivery (costs, cycle)

THE CMS ENGINEERING/MANUFACTURING FUNCTIONAL MODEL

The CMS Engineering/Manufacturing Functional Model defines the generic activities that all discrete parts manufacturers will perform to make a product, regardless of the type of product or the manufacturing technologies employed. The model provides a standard definition of the engineering and manufacturing activities that occur over the entire life cycle of a product. Certain functions, such as marketing, are defined only to the level of detail required to identify data flows that affect the engineering and manufacturing model.

The functions are defined to communicate to management how resources are being consumed within a business. The model also highlights those activities and tasks that may be considered non-value-added or drivers of cost and performance.

The model provides a basis for activity accounting. It can be used as a starting point to determine which activities are considered significant. It provides a tool to help identify and eliminate waste. Fifteen functions are identified. The following sections define and describe these functions as they apply to the CMS model.

1. Strategic Planning

The strategic plan defines the objectives and constraints for the company's operation. The important data flows required from the strategic plan are the corporate mission, a forecast of products, the competitive strategies, and the financial constraints.

Product Forecast specifies the market for the product for the next five or ten years. This forecast should be translated into the manufacturing resources required and should be compared to existing facilities and other resources.

Competitive Strategies describe how actively the company will compete in its markets. Strategies can be proactive, technology-responsive, or reactive. Strategies also define the planned functional structures of the company.

Financial Constraints determine the amount of money available for investment, given the product market forecast, the competitive strategies chosen, and the company's current and expected financial condition. A major piece of this puzzle is the changing money market and its effect on the cost of money during the product life cycle.

2. Basic Research and Development

Basic research and development are not linked to specific products. Their function is to develop new product features and capabilities, or to discover new manufacturing methods or technologies, to provide a competitive advantage. As new ideas are generated, they will drive future applied research and development. Basic research and development comprise product R&D and process R&D.

Product R&D includes research into new types of materials and product capabilities, for instance, replacing mechanical components with electronic components.

Process R&D includes research into new types of manufacturing processes, the application of new technologies, and the application of existing technologies in new forms.

3. Marketing

Marketing is taken to mean the total customer interface, from market research to sales. Marketing is the source of the data that drive many other functions. It includes market research, pricing, sales forecasts, input to the master production schedule requirements, and sales.

Market Research includes collecting and interpreting market data, market trends, and customer preferences.

Pricing is an analysis of internal factors (costs) and external factors (market data) to determine the appropriate price for a product.

Sales Forecasts project future product demand. This function relies heavily on data generated by market research.

Master Production Schedule Requirements involve the application of sales forecast (demand) and actual customer orders to internal resources to establish a schedule for producing the product.

Sales include the activities involved in generating customer orders.

4. *Product/Process Development and Maintenance*

Product development and maintenance include the activities required to define, design, develop, test, release, and maintain the complete description of the products to be produced. The information developed for use by the other functions of the organization is referred to as the product description.

Process development and maintenance activities are the planning, engineering, and technology selection required to prepare the organization and the physical facility to release the product to production management. The output of process development and maintenance consists of all plans, specifications, and directions required to implement the plan for production of the items in the product description.

Product and process development are highly interrelated and should be interactive. Modifications of plans and instructions (as in engineering change notices) are an output of product/process development and maintenance activities.

Product development includes conceptual design; preliminary design and testing; detailed design; design analysis, testing, and evaluation; release of the design to production planning; and bills of material.

Conceptual Design is the formulation and general statement of a product's description.

Preliminary Design and Testing is the first stage of design. It determines the product's feasibility and identifies its critical components. Models, mockups, and partial prototypes are created during this phase.

Detailed Design is the "detailing" stage of engineering. Each part is identified, and a complete prototype is built.

Design Analysis, Testing, and Evaluation include all the activities that support a rigorous review of the engineering prototype. Product features are measured against the original specifications. The product is compared against requirements for product development and maintenance, production quality control, and the facilities required for production.

Release of the Design to Production Planning occurs only after the design has been stabilized, tested, and evaluated by engineering.

Bills of Material are generated as the product is released to manufacturing. Data produced in this activity drive development of production and support schedules.

Process development includes project management, analysis, process planning, process engineering, and investment management.

Project Management provides the scheduling and organizational direction that controls production. Such activities as budgeting and reporting provide the data flow critical to this function.

Analysis refers to the monitoring and review of the ongoing production process, which provide data to support decision making.

Process Planning includes the activities necessary to classify the resources and operations employed in manufacturing (especially quality-control operations).

Process Engineering involves determining the industrial, mechanical, and electrical engineering procedures for actually making the product.

Investment Management is part of a product's process planning and development activity because it directly affects the selection and acquisition of the technology used to make the product.

5. Tooling and Production Programming

Tooling is the function that determines tool requirements, creates the tool design, and performs those activities necessary to prepare the tool for production. Ongoing tool control is also included in this activity. Tooling, more specifically, is the defining, procuring, storing, maintaining, inspecting, delivering, repair, and calibration of the physical tools required in production.

Production programming includes all programming that controls the operation of machines related to production and inspection. Production programming is generating and maintaining the programs (software) used in production, including such areas as NC/CNC/DNC and robotics.

6. Production Management

The production management function includes all activities required to manage and control the operation of the production process: production planning and control (systems), assignment of workers (allocation), shop-floor control (people), production monitoring, time charging, and financial control.

Production Planning and Control Systems (usually commercially available software) ensure a balance between resources and requirements. Programs typically include: capacity planning, material requirements planning, production planning, and inventory management.

Assignment of Workers matches work assignments to worker skills, based on production schedules. The primary manufacturing planning and control system includes the factory scheduling system.

Shop-Floor Control determines the number of people needed to strike a balance between resources and requirements: supervisors, schedulers, planners, expediters, and dispatchers.

Production Monitoring provides dynamic status information on production activities.

Time Charging is a reporting system that tracks labor by task and flags shortfalls due to absences.

Financial Control includes the traditional accounting functions: cost accounting, payroll, accounts payable, accounts receivable, fixed assets, and general ledger.

7. In-process Material Movement

Material movement includes the storage, distribution, and transportation of in-process inventory. It deals with such issues as automated material handling, material storage and retrieval systems, item identification, and in-process packaging.

In-Process Stores is the storage of WIP inventory.

Transport Material is the activity that moves materials from one operation to another.

WIP/Queue-Related Material Movement affects material related to in-process backlogs.

8. Production Operations

Production operations encompass the physical production activities that add value to the product, such as fabrication and assembly.

Fabrication is making discrete parts, which may or may not be components of larger assemblies.

Assembly includes the activities required to incorporate individual parts into complete assemblies or subassemblies.

Other production operations may be required, depending upon the complexity of the parts or the processes required to produce them.

9. Incoming Material Control

Incoming material control includes procurement, vendor tracking, receiving, incoming inspection, raw-material storage/distribution, and transport to the first manufacturing operation.

Procurement includes all the activities associated with buying materials: vendor qualification, purchase-order maintenance, vendor selection, vendor tracking, incoming receiving, and incoming inspection.

Raw-Material Storage is the control of raw-material inventory, movement, and storage.

Transport is the physical movement of raw material from receiving dock to stores to the first manufacturing operation.

10. Outgoing Material Control

Outgoing material control is responsible for finished-goods handling. It includes transport from the last manufacturing operation to stores, and the storage, packaging, shipping, and distribution of finished goods to the customer or distribution center.

Transport to finished goods from line to stores is the physical movement of products from the last manufacturing operation to finished-goods storage or shipping.

Finished-Goods Storage is the control of finished-goods inventory.

Shipping is preparing products for delivery and arranging the method for delivery to customers.

Distribution is the marketing or merchandising scheme for the products.

11. Production Quality Control

Production quality control is responsible for planning, implementing, and executing the quality plan developed for manufactured items.

Quality-Assurance Planning is the activity of setting specifications and tolerances, documenting procedures, and determining the type and location of inspection sites and equipment. These activities begin no later than process development. With many modern products (semiconductors and electronic products, for example), quality inspection factors are planned during the earliest product design stages and are sometimes manufactured into the product.

Quality-Control Activities are the actual checks, physical inspection, gauging, and testing done on the product.

12. Human Resources

The human resources function handles all activities related to the labor component of manufacturing, including personnel management, administration, union relations, training, compensation, and benefits administration.

13. Information Systems

Information systems provide data and computer technologies necessary to support and, in some cases, to perform the manufacturing process. It includes people, machines, and programs as required.

Personnel like supervisors, programmers, analysts, operators, and clerks provide service and support for information services.

Technology includes the hardware (equipment) and software (applications, systems, database, communications) required to deliver information where and when it is needed throughout the company.

14. Facilities Management

Various services are necessary to maintain a company's physical plant: maintenance, security, energy management, plant management, new plant construction, emergency assistance, and external compliance (regulatory services).

Maintenance includes the people, equipment, and services necessary to keep the plant and its machinery operational.

Plant Security ensures the safety of both the plant and the workers.

Energy Management includes the people, systems, and services necessary to control energy distribution and costs.

Plant Rearrangement and Construction is the function that renovates existing structures, arranges for equipment and personnel relocation, and builds new facilities as necessary to accommodate new products, processes, or technologies.

External Compliance includes those tasks associated with ensuring compliance with externally legislated or regulated issues, such as environment protection (EPA) and worker safety (OSHA).

15. Product Services

Product services maintain the product after delivery to the customer. They comprise installation, ongoing maintenance, warranty service, and spares inventory.

Installation is setting up the product for use at the customer's site.

Ongoing Maintenance includes those activities necessary to ensure that the product continues to work according to specifications after it is installed at the customer's site.

Warranty Service covers preventive maintenance and repairs performed during the product's warranty period.

Spares are parts held in inventory for the purpose of replacing broken or worn-out components of products previously sold to customers.

THE CMS MANUFACTURING PRACTICES PROFILE

The CMS Engineering/Manufacturing Functional Model describes the activities performed by discrete parts manufacturers. Using the CMS Functional Model as a baseline, this section describes a Manufacturing Practices Profile that illustrates how the characteristics of the functions in the model change as companies adopt new strategies and technologies. The functions will always be performed, regardless of the strategies and technologies employed. However, the techniques and the areas of responsibility of the functions may differ, depending upon a company's level of automation. This section defines the elements that change, how they change, and why they change. From this perspective, we can begin to understand the information requirements for each manufacturing environment. This understanding supports the guidelines for the CMS.

The major drivers of change in manufacturing are the proliferation of advanced manufacturing technologies and strategies (such as JIT/TQC, CAD/CAM, CIM), and the focus on eliminating non-value-added costs to gain a competitive advantage. Manufacturing environments in the CMS profile center on these catalysts of change. Levels of automation (environments) described in the profile include traditional manufacturing (the baseline), process simplification, islands of automation, computer-integrated manufacturing, and optimized manufacturing. Tables 3.1–3.15 summarize the CMS model functions within each of these environments.

Table 3.1
Strategic Planning

ENVIRONMENT	CHARACTERISTICS
Traditional Manufacturing	Marketing orientation. Role of manufacturing is to build products that conform to marketing requirements.
Process Simplification	Manufacturing becomes a competitive weapon and can be used to differentiate a company in the marketplace through elimination of waste, improved quality, and process reliability.
Islands of Automation	Use of automation to address problem and opportunity areas. Provides relatively low-risk approach for the application of new technology.
Computer-Integrated Manufacturing	Emphasis on integration of engineering and manufacturing activities to gain competitive edge through reduced costs, flexibility, responsiveness to customer, responsiveness to business opportunity.
Optimized Manufacturing	Competitive edge based on elimination of non-value-added costs and judicious use of automation. Product differentiation. Flexible view of "what business the company is in."

Table 3.2
Basic Research and Development

ENVIRONMENT	CHARACTERISTICS
Traditional Manufacturing	Emphasis on product R&D (features, appearance).
Process Simplification	Extensive analysis of current product/process engineering. Emphasis expanded to include advanced process engineering. R&D methodology for increased reliability.
Islands of Automation	Emphasis expanded to include extensive research into automated process technologies, advanced CAD, and Group Technology.
Computer-Integrated Manufacturing	Emphasis expanded to include developing integration technologies (CAD, CAM, MIS).
Optimized Manufacturing	Emphasis includes process engineering, enabling technologies, development of integrated decision-support systems, and integration.

Table 3.3
Marketing

ENVIRONMENT	CHARACTERISTICS
Traditional Manufacturing	Companies slot themselves into a market segment based on certain product features; then competition is based on price. Complex forecasting techniques used as hedge against long lead times. Field service emphasized.
Process Simplification	Competition based on reaction time, quality, reduction of non-value-added costs. Field reliability emphasized.
Islands of Automation	Competition based on flexibility, quality, decreasing labor costs through use of automation. More product features. Decreased lead time, increased responsiveness.
Computer-Integrated Manufacturing	Competition based on flexibility, increased throughput, reduction of labor cost through integration of information flow, and reduction of overhead. Product resistance to obsolescence.
Optimized Manufacturing	Competition based on price, quality, flexibility, throughput by: rationalization, elimination of waste, organization into flow line, automation, integration. Customized products. Increased international marketing. Increased market segmentation.

Table 3.4
Product/Process Development and Maintenance

ENVIRONMENT	CHARACTERISTICS
Traditional Manufacturing	Two separate and distinct functions with little interaction. Role of designer is to maximize design criteria. When complete, role of process engineering is to determine methods for manufacture. Primary emphasis is on product features. Drawings on paper, "hard" mockups, routings manually engineered. Product/process changes costly and slow.
Process Simplification	Design for producibility is a major concern, so product/process development becomes more integrated. Use of Group Technology, variant process planning. Product, process, and tools analyzed, simplified, and stabilized. Interaction with vendors/contractors in planning stage.
Islands of Automation	Sophisticated computer-based tools used to increase efficiency. Drawings maintained on computer, three-dimensional models take place of mockups, routings generated via CAPP. Product design for automation, Group Technology, and tool-management systems.
Computer-Integrated Manufacturing	Product and process engineering are merged into an operating team. Minimized cost/response time for product/process changes.
Optimized Manufacturing	Single process, including data, that allows for decisions resulting in lowest life-cycle cost. CIM overhead reduced. Close ties between engineering, manufacturing, and marketing.

Table 3.5
Tooling and Production Programming

ENVIRONMENT	CHARACTERISTICS
Traditional Manufacturing	Dedicated tools. Centralized tool cribs. Proliferation of tools. N/C programming is labor-intensive.
Process Simplification	General-purpose tools. Tools located near point of use. Use of specialized machines and tools often developed in-house to reduce setups.
Islands of Automation	Migrate from hard tools to computer tools (NC, CNC, or DNC). Some adaptive control. Production programming becomes important manufacturing resource. Hard tools located near point of use. Use of Group Technology for design and management. Software support reduces N/C programming effort.
Computer-Integrated Manufacturing	Increased use of DNC. All tools located near point of use. Automated tool management. Modular tools. Most NC programs generated automatically. Databases for part geometries and plant resources are combined.
Optimized Manufacturing	This function becomes integrated into the design process. Adaptive control is widespread.

Table 3.6
Production Management

ENVIRONMENT	CHARACTERISTICS
Traditional Manufacturing	Complex systems utilized to balance resources and demand (MRP, Infinite Series Planning, Capacity Planning). Many support personnel required to compensate for schedule changes, excessive material handling. Production monitoring and financial control occur at very finite level and require large databases (paper-controlled) to collect and report information.
Process Simplification	Fewer support personnel and systems needed, because focus is on elimination of problem rather than work-arounds. Less detailed transactions, production monitoring; financial postings occur through back flushing. Material movement is monitored for job-status reporting.
Islands of Automation	Bar code, optical scanners used to post production monitoring and financial control systems. Expert systems used for shop loading. Introduction of paperless systems. Modeling used to simulate and optimize flow.
Computer-Integrated Manufacturing	Planning and control systems become real-time as need for sophistication is diminished because production is triggered by demand. Line controllers also trigger posting of production monitoring and financial control systems. Worker assignment and time charging are no longer required, as direct labor is virtually eliminated. Allocation of labor and equipment based on expert modeling systems.
Optimized Manufacturing	Capacity management becomes a resource-planning function rather than a daily loading exercise.

Table 3.7
In-Process Material Movement

ENVIRONMENT	CHARACTERISTICS
Traditional Manufacturing	Overall goal is high utilization of machines, so items move many times over long distances; in-process storage occurs after each operation; movement occurs in large lots; methods are manual, forklifts.
Process Simplification	Occurs in small lots. Use of standard containers. Flow philosophy groups machines by part families to reduce distance traveled. Few in-process stores; attempt to keep inventory moving.
Islands of Automation	Automated storage and retrieval systems (AS/RS). Conveyors. Automatically guided vehicles (AGVs) for movement between operations. Use of standard containerization.
Computer-Integrated Manufacturing	Material-handling equipment integrated with scheduling and production systems. Virtual cells accomplished via sophisticated material-handling equipment that allows rapid movement between machines located at various areas of the plant.
Optimized Manufacturing	Focus on reduction in distance traveled, automated material handling. Elaborate storage systems no longer required.

Table 3.8
Production Operations

ENVIRONMENT	CHARACTERISTICS
Traditional Manufacturing	Labor-based. Smallest percentage of manufacturing lead time. Run large lots. Triggered by need to keep manufacturing resources busy. Like machines grouped together.
Process Simplification	Run small lots. Triggered by demand. Largely labor-based. Becomes a larger percentage of manufacturing lead time because move, queue, setup are reduced. Attempt to minimize all other components of manufacturing lead time. Machines grouped for families of parts. Constant review of processes for improvement of material flow.
Islands of Automation	Switch from labor-based to technology-based.
Computer-Integrated Manufacturing	Technology-based. Integration of all operations.
Optimized Manufacturing	A items—flow accomplished through dedicated cells. B and C items—flow accomplished through virtual cells. Lot size = 1. Integration of all activities.

Table 3.9
Incoming Material Control

ENVIRONMENT	CHARACTERISTICS
Traditional Manufacturing	Many vendors for same components, spread-out locations. Competitive bids, selection based on lowest price. Large deliveries, including safety stock. Customer inspects goods, often reworks defects. All items (except shortages) are routed to stockroom after passing inspection. Dock-to-stock lead time measured in days. Material ordered based on forecast.
Process Simplification	Few vendors—nearby; close business ties. Vendor certification. Source inspection. Material introduced directly to line. Replenishments based on demand. Emphasis on purchased part's role in life-cycle cost. Smaller, more frequent deliveries.
Islands of Automation	Electronic links to vendors. Automated storage/retrieval systems (AS/RS).
Computer-Integrated Manufacturing	Requirements automatically trigger vendor requisitioning system.
Optimized Manufacturing	JIT purchasing. Source Q/A. Electronic links to vendor; automatically generated requisitions.

Table 3.10
Outgoing Material Control

ENVIRONMENT	CHARACTERISTICS
Traditional Manufacturing	Build to forecast. Goods shipped from finished-goods stores. Large finished-goods stores require extra time for picking parts, complex priority rules. Many stockouts cause shipping delays. Distribution systems paper-intensive.
Process Simplification	Less need for finished-goods stores because of shortened lead times. Build to demand. Source inspection for customers.
Islands of Automation	Electronic links with customers.
Computer-Integrated Manufacturing	Electronic links with customers trigger production.
Optimized Manufacturing	Minimum time from last operation to customer acceptance.

Table 3.11
Production Quality Control

ENVIRONMENT	CHARACTERISTICS
Traditional Manufacturing	Separate quality-control departments. Inspection is a discrete operation. Quality is "inspected in." Lot size contains allowance for scrap, rework. Inspection and return by entire lot.
Process Simplification	Responsibility for quality is at source, built-in, not inspected-in. Goal of totally eliminating defects. Worker participation is encouraged. Operators check their own work. Quality circles. Tool statistics. Statistical process control (SPC). Design considerations: mistake-proofing, design for inspectability.
Islands of Automation	Use of automation to reduce defects through increased precision and tighter tolerances. Application of inspection technology to Q/C process. Individual devices log their own statistics. Information feedback loop within a cell. Vision systems.
Computer-Integrated Manufacturing	Automated inspection, often part of production operation. Integration allows for automatic rerouting of defects. Defects of 1. Rework cost model: a parameter-driven quality model that determines whether a part should be reworked or scrapped. The greater the integration, the less the need for traditional material requirements planning. In-line gauging: focus on preventing rather than catching first defect. Preoperation sensing devices determine optimal tolerance.
Optimized Manufacturing	Off-fall (production by-products) scrap is minimized, and yield continually improved through feedback to design group. Zero defects. No scrap, rework allowance in standards. Extensive automated inspection to prevent defects. Production operation and inspection are one step.

Table 3.12
Human Resources

ENVIRONMENT	CHARACTERISTICS
Traditional Manufacturing	Large numbers of direct workers. Manual skilled. Workers specialized because of functional training or union constraints. Compensation and fringes are major cost factors. Labor measured by individual or department efficiency. Large numbers of nontechnical support personnel. Labor-paced. Organizational redundancies caused by overlap of responsibilities.
Process Simplification	Major education effort and management commitment needed to instill JIT philosophy. Cross-training; cooperation. Measured on plantwide/cellwide basis. Large degree of worker involvement in problem solving. Support personnel reduced. Incentive programs. Quality circles. Focus on improving communications. Redundancies/overlap minimized.
Islands of Automation	Reduced direct labor through use of automation. Displacement of workers results in training/retraining issues (to use automated technologies). Upgrading of technical skills. Multifunction workers—fewer job classifications. Increased support staff (highly skilled) to maintain automation. Machine-paced. Management training required to encourage use of enhanced data in decision making.
Computer-Integrated Manufacturing	Direct labor (overseers) only to support many machines. Highly specialized staff to maintain production machines. Much computer expertise required. Factory designers: integration skills technical, yet high-level. Tools to boost productivity of support personnel: artificial intelligence, expert systems, fourth-generation programming languages. Environment requires great degree of discipline. Training/retraining issues. Management decisions have widespread and rapid impact because of integration: required fast-paced decision and policy changes.
Optimized Manufacturing	Decreased management and support layers through use of productivity tools. Use of direct labor only for operations where that is the optimal method. Short communication lines between managers and workers. Flatter organizational structure exposes upper management to immediate problems.

Table 3.13
Information Systems

ENVIRONMENT	CHARACTERISTICS
Traditional Manufacturing	Expensive; centralized. Long lead time for new software enhancements. Systems track and report at lowest level of detail. Data integrity is a major issue. Lack of integration. Reliability problems with older hardware.
Process Simplification	Decentralized, simplified. Increased communication needs. Data tracked at higher levels. Decreased lead time results in less need for detailed transactions. Strives to create an environment that does not require complex systems. End-user tools and generators to avoid MIS backlog.
Islands of Automation	Extensive use of computers in manufacturing and engineering functions. More hardware on the line measuring and controlling. Library of reusable code (cells). Multiple communications links, or local area networks (LANs).
Computer-Integrated Manufacturing	Internal controls issue. Controls virtually all activities of manufacturing. Heavy emphasis on communications and integration (rapid feedback to corporate MIS). Extensive support costs. Fault-tolerant systems (2 in 1). More code generated at source (design drives process plan, NC code). Decentralized factory floor. Centralized support applications (payroll, accounts payable). Global electronic data transfer. Move toward paperless operation: on-line presentation of data.
Optimized Manufacturing	All systems integrated and on-line. Data often tracked at detail level but reported at summary levels. Corporate standards and guidelines to control decentralized data processing (starts at Islands of Automation).

Table 3.14
Facilities Management

ENVIRONMENT	CHARACTERISTICS
Traditional Manufacturing	Layout by function: group like machines together. Maintenance as required. Centralized support function. Large space needed for storage of inventories. Inefficient plant layout causes excessive material movement. Few facilities-modeling and planning systems.
Process Simplification	Reduction in space requirements. Compressed layout based on Group Technology. Scheduled maintenance as part of production cycle. Cells based on product families. Flexible facilities. Facilities support is decentralized, often cell-independent. Minimal need for inventory storage; remaining storage more efficient. Building design for introduction of raw material directly to production. Facilities modeling and planning. Facilities introduced into strategic plan.
Islands of Automation	Layout for automation. Rewire plants for communications and isolated power. Increased design and planning support staff. Focused factories. Sophisticated modeling tools. Tie to strategic planning.
Computer-Integrated Manufacturing	Layout for automation. Large support staff. Fewer people = less need for people-related facilities. "Lights out" factories. Backup power (uninterrupted power supply). Transfer lines. Computers for energy management.
Optimized Manufacturing	Smaller facilities because of less inventory storage, compressed plant layout. Closed-loop environmental monitoring and feedback. Less support staff. Facilities planning integrated into product design.

Table 3.15
Product Service

ENVIRONMENT	CHARACTERISTICS
Traditional Manufacturing	Installation often complex because of product design. High warranty costs; quality problems. Maintenance of large inventory to support spares. Spares production is costly because of high EOQ.
Process Simplification	Higher quality = lower warranty costs. Shorter lead time reduces spares inventory. Spares production more economical because of lower EOQ. Higher customer-service levels.
Islands of Automation	Reliability models. Diagnostics via telephone lines. Systems to plan/schedule maintenance, spares inventory. Warranty tracking. Reduced support cost through better: product design, documentation. Improved maintainability.
Computer-Integrated Manufacturing	Increased flexibility reduces need for spares inventory. Logistics main driver of spares. Some customer-site spares inventory. Spares inventory. Electronic link to customers for diagnostics, some repair. Warranty performance information integrated into engineering, production, Q/C. Increased customer responsibility for repairs.
Optimized Manufacturing	Low warranty costs because of high product quality. Spares logistics supported by expert systems. Unified life-cycle engineering (producibility, reliability, maintainability, supportability).

QUALITY MANAGEMENT

This section explores the issues connected with quality management. While quality has become a major factor in increasing market share and profitability (often surpassing price in importance), many companies continue to focus on the correction of problems rather than on integrating quality into product design and development. Technologies such as statistical process control (SPC), mistake-proofing, total quality control, and the Taguchi method offer great promise for the reduction of non-value-added quality costs. If managers knew the costs of poor quality, they would be able to make better decisions regarding cost/quality trade-offs.

During the past decade, the automotive industry has shown the impact of quality on market share. However, in today's competitive markets, quality alone is not sufficient: continual quality improvement *and* cost reduction are necessary for a company's economic survival. Quality has many different implications in the United States. According to L. P. Sullivan, "Quality definitions are confused by such slogans as 'Do it right the first time,' 'Corporate commitment,' 'Excellence plus,' 'Quality mandate,' and so on. If you probe deeper into various company quality goals, you find that they usually translate into an objective to manufacture and ship parts that fall within engineering specification limits or local quality acceptance standards."[1]

U.S. manufacturers traditionally have used such tools as inspection after production and statistical process control to control quality during production. These on-line quality-control methods strive to keep the manufacturing process in statistical control and to reduce manufacturing imperfections in the product. When a problem is identified, its possible causes are analyzed. The typical approach to reducing the variation (and thereby improving quality) is to remove the cause. This can be, and often is, costly.

Quality motivation that focuses on conforming to specification can lead to major quality and cost problems. The practice of stating product and process characteristics in terms of tolerance intervals can cause a manufacturer to produce products of poor quality and reliability even if the individual parts are within tolerance intervals. Such a product may not perform satisfactorily, since parts on

---

1. Sullivan, "Reducing Variability," 16.

the lower limit do not always mate properly with adjacent parts on the upper limit ("tolerance stackup").

The final quality and cost of a manufactured product are determined primarily by engineering design and manufacturing processes. Off-line methods are quality-control and cost-control activities conducted during the product and process design stage to improve product manufacturability and reliability and to reduce life-cycle costs. Examples of off-line quality-control methods are design reviews, sensitivity analyses, prototype tests, accelerated life tests, and reliability studies.

One of the recent developments in off-line quality-control methods in the United States is the discovery of the work of Genichi Taguchi. Taguchi has promoted the use of statistical design-of-equipment methods for product design improvement. His methods allow an engineer to analyze a large number of variables and interactions among variables to achieve the highest quality with the least expenditure of time and money. "[His] strategy calls for making products and processes that are 'robust against noise' (product deterioration, manufacturing imperfections, and environment factors) by first removing the *effects* of causes instead of removing the *causes*. Consequently, products can be manufactured more uniformly and will perform more consistently in service under a variety of conditions."[2]

Taguchi has also defined the nebulous term *quality* via a loss function, so that it can be measured in terms of dollars *and* linked to the technology of the product. Taguchi's definition examines the loss to society from the time a product is shipped. All societal losses due to poor performance of a product are attributed to the quality of the product. The smaller the loss, the more desirable the product. Kackar has suggested that Taguchi's definition should be expanded to include the societal losses that occur while the product is being manufactured.[3] The loss function is a composite of all internal costs, warranty and field costs, the cost to the customer, and the cost to society.

For a company just starting to use the loss function, it is not important to represent the full loss to society (initially). When

---

2. Copp, "Japanese Quality Engineering Using Designed Experiments," 7.
3. Kackar, "Off-Line Quality Control," 176. Kackar, "Taguchi's Quality Philosophy," 22.

starting out, a company can use the internal costs plus warranty and field costs. As the company becomes more experienced, it can attempt to quantify the loss to the customer and, eventually, the loss to society.

While there is controversy over Taguchi's statistical methods, most agree that his loss function represents a solid contribution. Sullivan states, "The real power in the loss function is its impact on changing the way we think about quality and the methods we use to fund quality improvements that normally do not meet the traditional payback guidelines."[4]

High quality and low cost are not necessarily conflicting objectives. The Taguchi methods should not be viewed as goals but rather as tools to utilize as part of a company's overall approach to quality management. Through the appropriate combination of on-line and off-line quality-control techniques and the effective development of resources, a company can reduce waste and improve productivity. Quality can be a means of lowering manufacturing cost and improving a company's competitive position.

The Taguchi Philosophy

Taguchi's quality philosophy can be summarized in seven principles:

1. The loss a product causes to society is an important dimension of the product's quality.
2. Continuous quality improvement and cost reduction are necessary to remain competitive.
3. Quality-improvement programs must work to reduce variations in product performance.
4. A customer's loss is approximately proportional to the square of the difference between actual and designed performance.
5. Actual quality and cost are determined to a large extent by effort expended in engineering design and manufacturing process.
6. Performance variation can be reduced by exploiting the non-linear effects of product or process parameters on performance.
7. Statistically planned experiments can identify the product or process parameters that minimize performance variation.

---

4. Sullivan, "The Seven Stages of Company-wide Quality Control," 82.

The Taguchi Method

Taguchi supports his quality philosophy with a methodology. The aim of his method is to address the impact of quality on cost by focusing on three phases of production. All three phases occur during the engineering-design stage of a product's life cycle. The phases are system design, parameter design, and tolerance design.

System Design. A functional prototype design is produced. Taguchi's approach at this phase is to use the prototype to define the initial design's product or process parameters. These parameters become Taguchi's loss-control targets.

Parameter Design. Product or process parameters are identified in detail. Taguchi's method is to use simulation or experimentation to derive statistical information about the parameters. This information shows how the parameters impact loss. Thus, the experimental data can be used to minimize *expected* loss. The goal of parameter design, then, is to avoid actual loss by providing product and process data that can be used to develop a more stable, more reliable (higher-quality) product.

Tolerance Design. The amount of control the manufacturer will have over the parameters (hence, loss and quality) is determined. The approach here is to examine the effect of tolerances on the product:

Tighter tolerances = Higher product/process cost
Looser tolerances = Lower product performance/higher loss

The Taguchi method emphasizes the need to strike a balance between loss and costs. His approach makes it possible to measure and control such trade-offs. Furthermore, it emphasizes front-end design stages. The earlier a loss parameter can be identified, the better engineers can address the problem prior to actually incurring the loss (which happens only after sale).

Timeliness and scope are key elements in the Taguchi method:

▪ A small but measurable result that occurs early in the design phase is worth more in loss prevention than a larger result that occurs only after product release.
▪ A large number of small improvements spread over a large num-

ber of products or processes gives a greater cumulative effect on quality than a small number of large improvements.

Quality Accounting

There are three important dimensions of quality accounting: (1) performance to specifications, (2) design for quality, and (3) defect prevention.

Ensuring that products perform to specifications is primarily a function of the inspection process. Sophisticated technologies are being developed to improve the inspection process. Measures include scrap, rework, yields, and warranty. The primary advanced manufacturing technologies that affect performance to specifications include machine vision, statistical process controls, adaptive controls, automated testing and measuring equipment, and feature technology.

Designing for quality emphasizes the importance of the engineering function in designing products to minimize or prevent quality problems, by designing for manufacturability. The primary advanced manufacturing technologies that are available in designing for quality include computer-aided design, computer-aided testing, computer-aided engineering, computer-aided process planning, life-cycle analysis, artificial intelligence/expert systems, and feature technology.

A goal of defect prevention is to build the product correctly the first time. This goal focuses on the importance of the manufacturing process in preventing defects. Measures include scrap, rework, and yield. The primary advanced manufacturing technologies that affect defect prevention are just-in-time, automated processing and assembly systems, quality circles, in-line inspection, adaptive controls, machine-monitoring systems, and engineering change control systems.

REFERENCES

Copp, R. "Japanese Quality Engineering Using Designed Experiments." Prepared for Holley Carburetor Divison. Dearborn, MI: American Supplier Institute, 1984.

Kackar, R. N. "Off-line Quality Control, Parameter Design, and the

Taguchi Method." *Journal of Quality Technology* (October 1985): 176–188.

———. "Taguchi's Quality Philosophy: Analysis and Commentary." *Quality Progress* (December 1986): 21–29.

Kobayashi, K. "Quality Management at NEC Corporation." *Quality Progress* (April 1986): 18–23.

Sullivan, L. P. "Reducing Variability: A New Approach to Quality." *Quality Progress* (July 1984): 15–21.

———. "The Seven Stages of Company-wide Quality Control." *Quality Progress* (May 1986): 77–83.

CHAPTER 4

Accounting Models

T his chapter discusses cost accounting objectives, principles, and guidelines for developing an integrated cost management system. It also supplies case studies to illustrate alternative cost accounting methods in a typical factory.

A primary objective of a cost management system is to measure the cost of resources consumed in performing significant activities of the business. The company needs this information to make strategic business decisions, to plan and control routine operations, and to determine income and financial position. A cost management system should supply information on product costs, process costs, and activity costs, all traceable to management reporting objectives.

Topics examined in this chapter include product cost; pricing; reporting of product life-cycle, non-value-added, and other significant costs; improved cost center definition and allocation of costs; consistency with standards development, budgeting, and control; inventory valuation; technology accounting; and internal-control considerations.

MANAGEMENT REPORTING OBJECTIVES

The CMS Conceptual Design satisfies multiple reporting requirements: the same transaction may simultaneously supply cost information for several management reporting objectives, such as product cost, pricing, financial reports, tax reports, and project reports. Transactions will be captured once, associated with an activity, and subsequently traced to the desired reporting objective. It allows reporting to varying levels of detail, depending on management reporting needs.

Product Cost

Product cost data are used for a number of purposes within the company and externally. Traditional cost accounting systems have focused on inventory valuation and on complying with external reporting requirements. As the manufacturing environment has become more complex, product cost information takes on an even greater role in helping management to determine external and internal prices for products, decide on new product introductions and product abandonments, and identify improvement opportunities for product line and product mix.

The accuracy of product cost data can affect strategic decisions, with resulting long-term consequences for the company. One of the major goals of the CMS Conceptual Design is to provide more accurate product cost information for management decisions.

Pricing

Pricing is heavily influenced by prevailing market forces, and, in turn, the number of companies willing to offer a specific product is determined by their ability to make the product at a cost lower than the market-determined price. As a result, there is a strong interaction between pricing and cost decisions.

In the long run, of course, the price must be greater than the full product cost if a company is to remain in business. Too often, companies do not adequately trace all pertinent costs to the products that engender them. This results in incorrect pricing. For example, a large manufacturer offered a product that required significant setup cost. This cost was included as overhead rather than being traced to the product. Because the product was sold at a relatively low price, which did not reflect all pertinent costs, it captured the largest market share. The company believed this was a profitable product—until they analyzed the total of directly traceable costs. This is a common mistake, which often results in inappropriate product-retention or product-abandonment decisions.

It is the objective of CMS to develop decision-making tools to reduce the uncertainty of pricing decisions. One of the first steps in this process is understanding the factors that affect external prices:

▪ Type of market in which the firm operates
▪ Degree of competition and the availability of substitute products

- Demand and the elasticity of demand
- Nature of the product and any competitive advantages resulting from unique capabilities
- Customer loyalty and purchasing habits
- Percentage of the customer's total cost or purchased cost represented by the product
- Switching costs to change products
- Threat of forward/backward integration
- Regulatory requirements or implications—local, national, international
- Capital requirements to make the product at the desired volume
- Cost of making the product[1]

Pricing objectives for a product line may vary, depending on the circumstances. Profit, return-on-investment, market share, and total sales are typical objectives. In some cases, company strategy may dictate the pursuit of multiple objectives. The product market being served and the intensity of competition often influence the pricing policy chosen.[2]

During the product-introduction planning phase, a company determines the price that will enable it to capture a predetermined market share. The challenge is to develop a product that can be marketed profitably at the desired price, known as target cost. To support internal and external pricing decisions, two system capabilities are recommended for CMS: (1) A strategic plannning system with a competitive analysis module that includes market-related information. This will support what-if analyses for specific pricing decision models built by a company, since both cost-based and market-based data can be extracted for analysis. (2) The ability to provide full cost data. Product costs should be broken out into short-term and long-term components, and life-cycle totals should be accumulated. Fully traceable cost data and information regarding the long-term impact of capacity costs should be available. Imputed costs for inventory, product-development costs and marketing/distribution costs should also be reported for inclusion in product cost. Finally, the value-added approach for depreciation should be used for selected categories of assets (see the Technology Accounting section).

1. Porter, *Competitive Strategy.*
2. Gordon et al., *The Pricing Decision.*

Reporting Product Life-Cycle Costs

Life-cycle reporting will be used to provide a long-term picture of product-line profitability, feedback on the effectiveness of life-cycle planning, and cost data to clarify the economic impact of alternatives chosen in the design engineering phase. The CMS Engineering/Manufacturing Functional Model will serve as the basis for reporting product life-cycle costs. Depending on specific management needs, varying levels of detail may be captured for selected phases of the life cycle. Individual activity costs identified in the model may be kept in more detail, while costs for several activities relating to physical production may be summarized. Totals for the current period, year-to-date, and inception-to-date would be reported for each life-cycle category desired. Estimates prepared during life-cycle planning could be retained for comparison with the actual costs accumulated.

For an advanced manufacturer, technology has a significant impact not only on cost, but also on the competitive advantage of a firm. The consumption of this critical resource supports operational control and strategic decision making. Thus, determining accurate technology costs is essential for the effective management of the business.

Technology costs have increased as a percentage of total product cost, and most of the product cost is locked in before production. The techniques typically employed for calculating the cost of technology and allocating (instead of directly assigning) it to processes and products have distorted the results in technology-intensive environments. The increasing distortion of the information dictates that the cost of technology should be calculated differently and assigned more accurately to those activities that consume this resource.

It has been suggested that life-cycle reporting is not more widely used because it is not required for (external) financial reporting and because of the difficulty of determining the beginning or end of a product's life cycle. Life-cycle costing is the accumulation of costs for activities that occur over the entire life cycle of a product. Cost accounting systems have focused on reporting period costs associated with the physical production of the product (for example, recurring conversion costs), primarily for external reporting purposes. The CMS also should capture and report the nonrecurring costs of activities that occur during the product-development and product logistics support phases. This would provide a more accurate picture of true life-cycle costs.

Cost data should be accumulated across more than one year by product, function, activity, and cost element. Accounting-period expense costs, such as product-development, marketing, and distribution costs, must be assigned directly to a product (or allocated on an appropriate basis).

The CMS should maintain life-cycle budget information to permit a comparison of budgeted versus actual costs. This helps monitor the effectiveness of life-cycle planning. Chapter 5 discusses life-cycle management issues in detail.

A value-added approach to depreciation is suggested for certain categories of fixed assets. For these categories, the asset value should be expanded to reflect the ownership cost of the technology, which would include acquisition cost, adjustments to current or replacement cost, and cost of capital to finance the asset. Costs of owning the asset should be charged to products based on production usage rather than allocated over a fixed time (standard depreciation). The technological life of the asset instead of the book life should be used, and the value added by the technology should be charged to products past the asset-recovery period if the asset continues in production (see the Technology Accounting section). With the value-added approach, depreciation charges will be variable rather than fixed costs. The adjustment to current cost or replacement cost, the cost of capital employed in financing, and product charges after the original service life has expired each should be detailed separately. This would allow them to be included in management reports and then to be added back for external reporting.

Reporting Non-Value-Added and Other Significant Cost Elements

Product cost reports should be expanded to provide visibility of non-value-added costs. This means that product cost data must be organized by cost element and must be split into value-added and non-value-added totals. Cost elements should be chosen to highlight items traditionally included in overhead (or excluded because they are not necessary for external reporting). Examples of such costs are scrap/rework/warranty, engineering changes, service-center costs (industrial engineering, maintenance, data processing), inventory, capacity, asset holding costs, technology, and marketing/distribution.

Many companies today capture and report costs associated with scrap, rework, warranty, engineering changes, and service-center work. However, it is anticipated that some companies may need to charge these costs more directly than in the past to minimize the potential distortion caused by allocations. Other costs such as inventory and capacity will probably be new cost elements or will be calculated differently. Capacity costs that can be associated with a specific product line should be segregated from common capacity costs. The cost of excess capacity or of capacity limitations should also be detailed.

In the past, the holding cost of assets has been included in overhead. An imputed cost for receivables, raw-material inventory, work-in-process inventory, and finished-goods inventory should be charged to products as production expenses for management reporting purposes. These expenses must be financed through internal cash or external debt and equity. Therefore, they represent an im-

Figure 4.1
WIP Inventory Value Versus Time

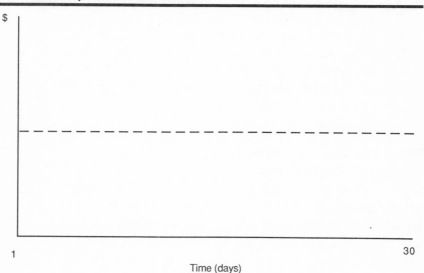

Figure 4.2
Average WIP Inventory Value Versus Time

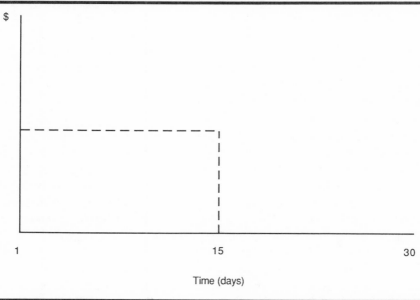

Time (days)

portant manufacturing cost. These costs should be kept separately so that they can be added back for external reporting purposes.

Consider, for example: the imputed cost of WIP. There is a direct relation between WIP and manufacturing lead time. Assume that

> Product A standard cost = $100
> Manufacturing lead time =   30 days
> Production quantity   =   100 units
> Production begins only on first day of the month

This product's WIP inventory value would be

$$100 \text{ units} \times \$100/\text{unit} = \$10,000$$

On any day of the month. A chart of WIP inventory value versus time would look like the one shown in Figure 4.1. If manufacturing lead time were reduced by 50 percent (to fifteen days), the average WIP inventory value would also be reduced by 50 percent (it would average $10,000 for the first fifteen days and $0 for the last fifteen days) (see Figure 4.2). Imputed interest can be charged to products using lead time as the basis. This relationship can be expressed as

$$\text{WIP cost/unit} = \text{Standard cost} \times \text{Lead time} \\ \times \text{Inventory carrying cost} \\ (\text{Imputed cost rate})$$

IMPROVED COST CENTER DEFINITION AND TRACEABILITY OF COSTS

To provide more accurate product cost information, improved approaches are required in cost center definition, direct traceability of costs, number of overhead rates, and basis of allocation. It is anticipated that more cost centers and cost pools will be established than is commonly practiced today to minimize potential distortions. Direct traceability of costs to specific manufacturing processes or products is recommended where practical.

The practice of using a plantwide overhead rate or a single overhead rate for a group of separate departments should be discontinued in most cases. The basis for applying overhead should be evaluated for each overhead rate that is developed. For those manufacturing processes that are manual operations or where labor paces the process, direct labor will remain the basis for applying overhead. Companies adopting just-in-time or continuous-flow production processes may use material dollars as an allocation basis. However, in heavily automated environments, machine hours probably will be the basis for applying overhead to manufacturing processes.

It is recommended to charge all manufacturing and support costs *directly* to the specific manufacturing processes or products where practical. This reduces the number of allocations and potential distortion. Where direct charging is infeasible, allocation bases using machine hours or material dollars will provide a partial solution to restructuring overhead rates. Understanding and predicting overhead cost-behavior patterns has been an elusive problem. Many types of overhead cost still appear to be fixed or to have no relation to these bases. Appropriate bases for applying overhead may be chosen by understanding drivers for these activities.

The recommended changes will result in significant departures from Generally Accepted Accounting Principles. Two distinct product cost reporting applications will result: one for internal management needs, another for external reporting.

Cost Centers, Cost Elements, Allocation Techniques, and Chart of Accounts

Cost centers, cost elements, and allocation techniques provide the framework for accumulating input data and for assigning or allocating costs to specific management reporting objectives. They represent the three primary, interdependent components of the accounting model, and they provide cost information needed to support reporting and control requirements.

Cost Centers. These centers mirror organizational structure. They are used to accumulate costs incurred in various engineering, support, and manufacturing activities. The degree to which the cost center structure of a firm coincides with the CMS Engineering/ Manufacturing Functional Model (see Chapter 3) will depend on how closely the organizational units correspond to the generic activities represented by the model. If there is little correlation, activity-based cost accumulation and reporting will be necessary to report costs for key activities performed by different organizational units.

Cost Elements. Cost elements designate the types of cost (labor, material, services, supplies). Cost elements will differ depending on the nature of the company's organization, its function, and its existing conventions. The descriptions of cost elements presented in this chapter include examples for several functions.

Allocation Techniques. These are the methods used to assign costs that cannot be identified specifically with a management reporting objective. An allocation process assigns costs that have been accumulated in a cost pool to a particular management reporting objective. Allocation techniques must be flexible. The sequence and basis of cost allocations within the cost center structure should change as the causal or beneficial relations among cost centers and activities change with respect to management reporting objectives. A causal relation is used to improve the use of economic resources and motivation. Some costs can be assigned directly (without allocation), while other costs will be allocated on such bases as direct-labor hours/dollars, machine hours, throughput time, transactions handled, number of setups, distance traveled, square footage, material dollars, and number of employees.

In moving toward optimized manufacturing, a company's organizational structure, manufacturing processes, and cost-behavior patterns will change. CMS must be flexible enough to respond to these changes. The cost center structure, cost elements, and allocation techniques must change to provide the cost information necessary to manage business activities effectively.

Chart of Accounts. The chart of accounts must be structured so that cost centers and cost elements can be added or removed easily as the company's organization, technology, and cost behavior change. When a new technology is introduced, more detailed information may be required to monitor the effects on cost and to diagnose problems. After the affected process stabilizes, less detailed information may suffice. As organizational realignments occur to accommodate changes in technology or management philosophies, it may become necessary to expand or contract the number of cost centers or to change the composition of cost elements to achieve the desired cost visibility.

Traditionally, companies have embedded the relation between organizational and cost center structures in the chart of accounts. Costs are collected for established "departments." But this organizational emphasis creates problems when management needs cost information for activities that cross departmental boundaries (e.g., costs of quality, purchase orders). Also, an organizational chart changes over time and may not accurately indicate the activities performed by a given individual or group at a particular time.

There are several approaches to capturing activity information. One approach is to expand the chart of accounts to include activities. A second approach is to structure cost centers to be synonymous with activities. The cost elements classify the type of resource consumed by the activity. Significant activities can be defined using a Pareto distribution (80 percent of the total work of the organization consists of 20 percent of the total activities). At most companies, the chart of accounts is a mix of organizational and activity accounts. The number of significant activities for any manufacturer would not be appreciably more detailed than is captured today in most charts of accounts.

The CMS Engineering/Manufacturing Functional Model is recommended as a basis for summarizing activity costs. The manufacturing processes can be classified as activities in the function labeled "perform production operations." Each manufacturing process can be associated with one or more cost centers. This allows the system to accommodate different types of automation and technologies. A manufacturing-process cost center could include a single machine, a group of like machines, a cell, a flexible manufacturing system, or an activity such as assembly, forging, and heat-treating.

Cost Center Definition

Cost centers should be established for organizational units and should consist of resources dedicated to similar activities. Cost centers provide the basic CMS units for capturing cost information. They accumulate costs that are assigned directly to the cost center or that were initially charged to a higher-level cost pool and then allocated to the cost center.

Defining cost centers is an important step in the development of a cost management system. Unique for each company, cost centers should be determined by management after considering the following questions: Which cost centers will provide the necessary information for strategic decisions or long-term projects needed to achieve company objectives? Which cost centers will provide the desired *operational* information needed to control costs (overhead, in particular) and to measure performance of: manufacturing processes and individuals? Which cost centers most logically fit the facility in terms of physical layout, product flow, and technology? Which cost centers will be consistent with the expected cost-behavior pattern? Which cost centers will provide the framework for the most accurate cost allocation to the final cost objective? Which approach provides the best cost-benefit relation (detail versus summary)?

Careful attention to the definition of cost centers is required to ensure that all the desired data are captured at the correct level of detail. Cost center definition should use the following guidelines.

Segregate Different Processes. Different manufacturing processes should be segregated into separate cost centers. For example, machining operations should not be combined with assembly operations.

Aggregate Families of Similar Machines. When a manufacturing process is performed on similar types of machines that have similar capabilities and costs, the entire family of machines should be treated as a single cost center.

Isolate Individual Machines. When significant differences exist between machines in a manufacturing process, either in terms of capabilities or of cost-behavior patterns, each machine should be treated as a separate cost center (for example, conventional machining versus DNC machining).

Base Cost Centers on Group Technology (GT). When a process contains a cell with related equipment that can be thought of as a complex single machine, it may be appropriate to treat the cell as a single cost center. Typically, the machines in the cell are functionally dissimilar (lathes, drills, material handling) but the process is one total system.

The basis for analyzing the appropriateness of a GT-based cost center is the number of machines used by each component in the family of parts. If the number of machines used by each component drops significantly below the average number of machines used for any one component, then it can attract an abnormally high overhead cost, since it had to help pay for machines that were not used by it. Also, in the case where two components are produced in parallel in a cell (parallel working), each family of components is helping to pay for machines used at the same time by other families of components, and vice versa. It could be argued that if the cell were properly constructed for a given family of parts, there would not be a notable difference in machine utilization for components within that family.

In practice, there are situations where components that use only one or two machines will be processed through the cell. While these components do not fit into standard family groups for which the cell was established, it may be necessary to include them because of specialized operations required (such as bending or gear-cutting), for which there are limited facilities. Because of the high cost of such machines and the typically low use, the machines are usually located in the cells that make the most use of them. Those components that also require this facility (but that are produced in another cell) must be transported to the cell with special equipment, resulting in inordinately high overhead costs for these components.

Labor costs can pose another problem, since there are cases where one person operates machines in different cells. This is particularly likely with the newer automatic-cycle machines. Also, each family of components in a cell can require a different number of machines and people. If a standard costing system is used, the optimum labor ratio can be incorporated into the standards for each family of components.

In summary, using cells as cost centers can create the following problems: Components using less machine time than other parts in a cell can attract high overhead; parallel working can attract high overhead; labor becomes indirect and difficult to trace to products; shared labor cannot be costed adequately. In non-flow-line cells the approach of treating a cell as a single cost center may not be successful. To decide how best to divide a cell requires studying the cell's work flow and machine usage. The effort required is a function of the number of components processed.

Assign Cost Center Responsibility to a Specific Individual. Only one person should be responsible for a cost center, but one person can be responsible for more than one cost center. This allows good control of cost accumulation and reporting.

Direct Traceability of Costs

Costs should be assigned directly to the lowest practical management reporting level. *Simultaneously*, they should be identified to the cost center and other known management reporting objectives when this is cost effective. This reduces the potential distortion that can result from the allocation process.

Cost centers should be established at a level that facilitates cost control and that results in the direct assignment or accurate allocation to the final management reporting objectives. Ideally, the cost center structure should be sufficiently detailed to assign costs directly to the desired management reporting objectives, capture and report significant cost elements at a level where they can be controlled, and accumulate homogeneous costs in cost pools for allocation to a reporting objective.

As a company moves toward optimized manufacturing, cost-behavior patterns will change. In such cases, a company needs to gain more visibility and control of costs typically classified as indirect (and included in manufacturing overhead). Costs that have traditionally been viewed as fixed overhead costs (and collected plantwide or at group-level cost pools) must be directly assigned to products that use the overhead when it is cost-effective to do so.

When equipment is dedicated to a specific product, or a support area is dedicated to a specific manufacturing process or product, transactions should be charged simultaneously to the cost center and to the product, the process, or both. This direct assignment of traceable costs removes the distortion that would be caused by using global allocations. For key support functions within the firm (such as industrial engineering), direct traceability of costs can be improved by implementing a service-center concept. The intent is to capture the cost of significant activities and charge them directly to the projects, processes, and products that use them. Of course, reporting minor tasks is not required for all support personnel. However, the cost of significant activities should be traced directly to specific manufacturing processes or products rather than allocated.

A costing system based on transactions volume may be a desirable alternative to an extensive activity-based time-reporting system. Transactions systems are often easier for a user to understand than some time-based systems. To be effective, the costing system should calculate a service charge for a transaction that is appropriate to the organizational unit. The cost per unit would be updated periodically. Not all applications adapt easily to transactions costing. Some combination of charging systems may be required. But, while transactions costing may not be easy to implement, it allows easier forecasting of costs and demonstration of productivity gains (when the unit price is lowered).

When direct assignment of costs is not possible or economical, cost pools should be established to accumulate homogeneous types of costs and allocate them to the desired management reporting objectives.

Number of Overhead Rates

In many companies, the number of overhead rates will need to be expanded to minimize product cost distortions. The use of a single, plantwide overhead rate should be discontinued except in a labor-intensive environment where machine tools are general-purpose, simple and inexpensive, and used to make only a single product. Where the manufacturing process consists of several different steps, separate cost centers and cost center overhead rates should be established to achieve more accurate product costs. Similarly, using a common overhead rate for a group of separate cost centers should be discouraged. Where the manufacturing process or products pass through the cost centers in relatively the same proportion with regard to the allocation basis, an overall burden rate would provide adequate product costing. If a piece of equipment is used only by specific products, only those products should absorb the cost of the equipment. The cost should not be averaged across all products.

Overhead rates should be developed for individual machines where significant differences exist between functions or machine costs. A single overhead rate can be used for a family of machines when similar types of machines produce similar parts with approximately the same process time. Machines in this category are characterized by similar capabilities and cost-behavior patterns. A single overhead rate may be applicable in Group Technology applications, where a process contains a cell with related equipment that can be thought of as a complex single machine.

A single overhead rate is appropriate if the facility produces a single product or multiple products that each receive the same level of effort. Multiple overhead rates are needed to reflect different cost-behavior patterns, routing variations, and volume patterns.

The relative volume of parts flowing through a cost center can affect the accuracy of allocations significantly. In situations where both high- and low-volume parts are processed in an area, assigning overhead with a single rate can result in the high-volume parts subsidizing the low-volume parts.

Basis of Allocation

Cost allocations should reflect causal relations between the cost pool and the management reporting objective. The process of assigning cost to management reporting objectives should be based on rules that emphasize the most appropriate cause-and-effect relation. Where causal relations are not discernible, allocations should reflect the benefits received. Implementation of this concept will require, in most cases, the use of multiple allocation bases in the business unit.

As more detailed cost centers and overhead rates are developed, the company must determine the appropriate bases for applying the overhead and ultimately allocating costs to products and processes. Cost-behavior patterns must be understood; direct labor no longer will be the appropriate basis in many cases. For labor-paced manufacturing, it is anticipated that the basis for developing the overhead rate will remain actual or standard labor hours. However, as more facilities become automated, a significant portion of total product cost shifts to technology-related costs. As the controlling factor shifts from people to machinery, value-added approaches to depreciation should be used to better match the cost of technology to products and processes. Allocation bases used for depreciation must be revised accordingly (see the Technology Accounting section).

Costs accumulated in higher-level cost pools and allocated to service centers, functions, or manufacturing processes must be examined individually to determine an allocation basis that best represents the benefits received or the cause of the charge. For these costs, traditionally known as overhead, direct labor, direct material, or machine hours may not provide an adequate basis for explanation and control. An activity basis like transactions volume or services rendered might prove superior to the traditional bases.

Cost behavior is dictated by cost drivers, those activities or decisions that are significant determinants of cost. A firm must determine which activities or events cause overhead costs to fluctuate. Some examples of cost drivers are inventory, space utilization, plant layout, transactions, engineering change notices, schedule changes, forecast accuracy, setups, and scrap/yield/rework.

Companies must identify drivers for cost centers and cost pools and implement flexible cost management systems to keep allocation bases current and accurate. Understanding the drivers will provide a good basis for monitoring and controlling costs. As a company moves toward optimized manufacturing, it will be a combination of automated and manual processes. Different levels of automation will exist in most manufacturing facilities as new technologies are implemented and existing ones phased out. Cost-behavior patterns will change. CMS must be flexible enough to handle different types of allocation bases for various cost centers and cost pools over time.

STANDARDS DEVELOPMENT AND BUDGETING CONSIDERATIONS

Costs should be accumulated consistent with the need to support standards development and budgeting. These activities assist management in planning and controlling operations. They include monitoring the financial and operational performance of activities to gauge their effectiveness; monitoring and controlling activities and drivers to understand the cost of associated waste; planning resource use for future activities; identifying potential areas for investments in new technology; and determining whether projected benefits from a new technology actually are being realized.

Standards Development

Standards are predetermined measures that relate resources or costs to products, organizational units, or other cost objectives. Each standard is designed to yield a benchmark—a point of reference for measuring performance—that reflects the expected relations between costs and objectives.

Standards are applicable to all the business functions of a manufacturing company, except in custom-shop operations where almost no processing patterns are ever repeated. In general, most operations can be organized and monitored so as to develop standards for use in planning, budget preparation, pricing, performance evaluation, and cost control. Standards and standard-cost information can be used without necessarily setting standards for all input elements or using a formal standard cost accounting system.

Standards can be expanded to provide additional management information on product costs. Standards must include additional data elements for calculating new cost details to be reported to management via revised product cost reports: value-added versus non-value-added costs, imputed cost of raw materials, imputed cost of WIP and finished-goods inventories, imputed cost of receivables, technology financing costs, and cost of excess capacity or capacity constraints.

The cost effects of capacity constraints must be reported to management. Flexible standards may be required in specific manufacturing environments. Capacity can be maximum (24 hours per day, seven days per week), normal (average actual, based on a historic period), or optimal (the mix of run time and idle time that best accomplishes operational goals).

The availability of automated tools and techniques during the design process will allow greater flexibility in choosing design alternatives to minimize total life-cycle cost. Once the design is finished, an "optimal" standard cost can be developed, based on the best routing for the facility at optimal capacity. Capacity constraints (lack of capacity or failure to properly maintain existing capacity) and multipurpose equipment can have a major impact on the actual routing employed and the resulting cost structure, particularly in manufacturing environments where the total production time is relatively long (weeks and months rather than days). The additional cost associated with these capacity constraints is often lost in the variance analysis. In relatively stable manufacturing environments the cost associated with capacity constraints could be calculated as the difference between the "optimal" standard cost and the actual cost. The difference could be segregated by causal factor and by affected manufacturing process for management reporting.

An "optimal" standard would represent state-of-the-art manufacturing conditions based on today's known technologies. The "expected" standard would reflect the existing conditions in the facility today. Actual costs could be compared to expected standards to measure performance under existing conditions. A second comparison could then be made with the optimal standard to reflect the nonproductive costs incurred. Expected standards could be based on historical cost trends, while optimal standards could be based on the optimal processes and what-if costs captured at the lowest practical level and rolled up to the appropriate reporting and measurement levels.

Cost control in the future will place increased emphasis on the use of optimal standards. This will require a heightened management awareness of the process of moving from current-trend data to optimal standards.

Budgeting

A budget is a managerial tool that translates the goals and objectives of the organization into a financial plan of action. After the selection of alternatives with regard to products, pricing, and capacity that are consistent with company strategy and the forecast demand requirements, the budgeting process requires management to develop a comprehensive picture of the expected operations.

When used for planning, budgets are normally static. Budgets are developed for an anticipated level of activity, with some sensitivity analysis to determine the effects of costs that vary from the plan if the activity level changes. Detailed departmental operating expense budgets serve as an important input for developing cash-flow requirements during the budgeting cycle and later for evaluating individual performance.

Performance is measured as a comparison of budgets to actual cost. As an area becomes increasingly automated or decentralized, the degree of control that an individual has over activity levels, the staffing, and the costs charged to that person's responsibility area may decrease.

A flexible budget recognizes that plans and schedules change. It compels operating managers to realize that they cannot earn their budget by maximizing production. Instead, their budget is based on activity levels required to satisfy external market demands for the product. Flexible budgeting encourages the operating manager to be sensitive to changes in activity levels and to manage costs for the appropriate activity levels. As companies progress toward optimized manufacturing, the effects of a pull system will increase the fluctuation of activity levels for many assets, since the philosophy of maximizing asset use will change to producing only what is needed.

The traditional characteristics of fixed and variable must be reviewed in light of the life-cycle approach. As companies automate, a larger percentage of costs shifts from variable to fixed. Costs previously viewed as variable may be fixed over the product life cycle. Expensive equipment may use dedicated labor teams and specialists to program and maintain the hardware and software. Cost-behavior patterns will become more complex with regard to overhead costs. Even the use of machine hours will reveal no cause-and-effect relation in many cases. Historical accounting data may not prove as useful as they have done in the past for predicting cost-behavior patterns, particularly if the computed cost is based on invalid assumptions.

Controlling overhead costs where they are generated requires the ability to predict costs that will be incurred for different activity levels. This implies flexible budgeting techniques and the use of standards that use key variables or cost drivers for predicting cost behavior, whenever these variables or drivers can be identified. Standards also must be modified to allow for additional data elements and calculations required to improve prediction of overhead costs. Theoretically, this approach could be used for each area of responsibility.

Nonfinancial measures will become increasingly important as a measure of performance in an advanced manufacturing environment. These measures will relate results to quantities planned and practical capacities established. Flexible-budgeting system capabilities must be expanded to incorporate these capabilities.

INVENTORY VALUATION

An important objective of the cost accounting process has been inventory valuation, which is the monetary measurement of inventory quantities using specific unit costs. Inventory valuation is required for interim internal financial reporting, external financial reporting, and short-term and annual planning of profitability and cost requirements. Improper inventory valuation can lead to major book-to-physical inventory adjustments, changes in cost-of-sales, and changes in profit or loss.

Generally, inventory valuation can be accomplished by either of two basic accounting approaches, regardless of the cost collection system used or the management reporting approach. The most common approach to inventory valuation is to establish a beginning inventory balance, and to accumulate the cost incurred in work-in-process to arrive at an ending inventory valuation and cost-of-sales. The ending inventory valuation becomes the starting point for the next period. Physical inventories are required only to check the process and to verify that the system is operating properly. The second approach is to obtain an ending inventory valuation by costing a physical inventory count. Purchases, issues, direct production labor, and overhead applied during the period are charged directly to cost-of-sales. Cost-of-sales and inventory value on the balance sheet are adjusted to reflect the new inventory valuation that was determined using the physical inventory.

As a company moves toward optimized manufacturing, the cost management system should be expanded to identify the holding costs of inventory (a non-value-added cost). This should encourage changes in the manufacturing environment to eliminate waste. Work-in-process inventory should be reduced significantly. The opportunity exists to reduce raw-materials and finished-goods inventories even further by integrating the production process backward to suppliers and forward to customers. In this environment the inventory-valuation problem is simplified.

Many people, particularly JIT enthusiasts, believe that simplification of inventory valuation will result from focusing on the control of total manufacturing costs rather than on valuing individual products. One proposed approach is known as just-in-time costing. In contrast to work-order accounting, the direct materials are posted directly to a "raw and in-process" account as they are received. All other costs are charged using a back flushing technique, in which completions trigger the relief of inventory, using the bill of materials to determine the items and quantities that should be deducted. These changes result in the absence of a separate account for raw-material inventory, the absence of work orders, and direct labor being treated as factory overhead.

As inventory levels decrease from JIT and other operational changes, the process of inventory valuation is simplified. The implementation of a pull system will greatly reduce WIP inventory. The use of standardized containers will permit easy determination of quantities. Physical inventory counts of WIP at the end of any given period will become practical or, in some cases, may not be required where there is little WIP at the end of any period. As a company adopts a philosophy of working closely with its suppliers, it will be able to synchronize receipt of raw-material inventory with production demands. Similarly, finished-goods inventory will be decreased and inventory obsolescence reserves will be reduced as the company manages its production to meet its customer requirements. The facility will begin to resemble a process-flow environment.

In a low-inventory, high-throughput environment one approach to inventory valuation is to charge purchases, issues, and conversion costs directly to cost-of-sales. The cost-of-sales and inventory value in the balance sheet would be adjusted to reflect the new inventory valuation that was determined using the physical inventory. This approach obviously represents an ideal situation—a process-flow environment in the entire facility—that many companies may not achieve all at once.

A sequential approach is recommended. Once a company has reduced its WIP inventory to a small amount, it would charge the material issues and conversion costs directly to finished-goods inventory. At the end of the period, a physical count of inventory or standardized containers can be made on the shop floor and a standard cost can be applied to obtain the value of WIP inventory. A journal entry would be made to relieve finished-goods inventory and to charge WIP inventory. Raw-material and finished-goods inventories would be valued as in the traditional approach. The major benefit would be the improved accuracy of the WIP inventory valuation, which reduces the need for obsolescence and inventory-adjustment reserves. Also, as the number of WIP units declines, there will be a decrease in the number of transactions to be recorded.

The next step would be to make month-end physical counts of raw-material and finished-goods inventories. This would be possible only after a synchronized flow has been established with suppliers and customers. Then the company can record materials purchased and conversion costs directly to the cost of goods sold. Using standard costs and the quantities counted, it would be possible to calculate the value of each of the inventories and to back this out of cost of goods sold.

TECHNOLOGY ACCOUNTING

The goal of technology accounting is to match better the "true" cost (or economic cost) of technology to the products that use the assets. This approach requires several departures from current cost accounting practices. First, more technology-related costs than is customary will be associated with products. Second, these costs will be matched to products using a value-added approach rather

Table 4.1

	TRADITIONAL	VALUE-ADDED
Technology cost	Purchase price + Startup cost − Residual value	Purchase price + Startup cost + Interest + Current-cost adjustment + Risk premium − Residual value
Basis for allocation	Fixed-time	Production usage
Recovery period	Useful or allowable life	Indefinite: depreciation continues after original recovery period
Product cost	Fixed	Variable

than including them in overhead. For management accounting purposes, it is important to understand that the total cost of technology includes acquisition cost, adjustments to current cost or replacement cost, and cost of capital employed to finance the acquisition. These ownership costs should be estimated for the useful life of each major asset and, based on changes in performance relative to current technology, should be adjusted annually. Today, only the acquisition cost is included in the depreciation calculation and asset costs are rarely adjusted after the original estimates.

Technology accounting places more emphasis on the use of value-added approaches rather than the (currently) predominant fixed-time methods. The value-added approach to depreciation has many similarities to, and differences from, the current approaches. Some of the important differences between technology accounting and present cost accounting practices are shown in Table 4.1. To determine value added, we first determine the level of cost accumulation and allocation (type of asset, level of control) and then compute the technology cost basis (value, recovery base, assignment methodology).

Determining the Level of Cost Accumulation and Allocation

Two important objectives of a cost accounting system are to accumulate manufacturing costs and to assign those costs to the product. To meet this objective successfully, it is important to use a technique that accurately represents the value added to each product. The objectives of technology accounting are to capture all the technology-direct costs and to minimize later allocations that result in product cost distortion. Figure 4.3 depicts the levels of a typical manufacturing organization where costs are accumulated and then allocated at lower levels, eventually at the product level. This is accomplished by using a hierarchical structure, whereby the costs are assigned first to the organizational unit where the cost is incurred and then to the cost generator. A cost generator represents the cause of the technology-direct cost. For example, a manufacturing process technology such as a five-axis NC machine is acquired to support production of specific products or product families. The technology generator is the product or family for which the five-axis NC machine was acquired. Remove the products and you remove the need for the machine.

The key to technology accounting is to trace technology costs directly to products. A wide variety of assets are currently employed in factories, and this fact does not change with the introduction of automation. Consequently, several different methods of accounting must be employed to trace technology costs to products. To provide a framework for discussion of the various accounting treatments available, it is necessary to classify capital assets into broad categories representative of the typical manufacturing environment. These categories are summarized in Table 4.2.

The corporation and plant level of allocation is applicable to those technologies that support a manufacturing facility or division as a whole but that cannot be identified with a specific manufacturing process. Costs of such technologies should be segregated into a general and administrative (G&A) expense pool, which is not directly allocated to production or included in product cost, and service centers, whose total costs are allocated to the various plants or business activities based on either specific usage data or a surrogate basis, such as square footage. Examples of corporate and factory-level allocations are administrative services, business computer operations, and plant/corporate management and administration.

Business activities support the production activities. Some of the activities are directly assignable to specific manufacturing processes, while others may be allocated to manufacturing processes using a surrogate basis.

Figure 4.3
Cost-Assignment Hierarchy

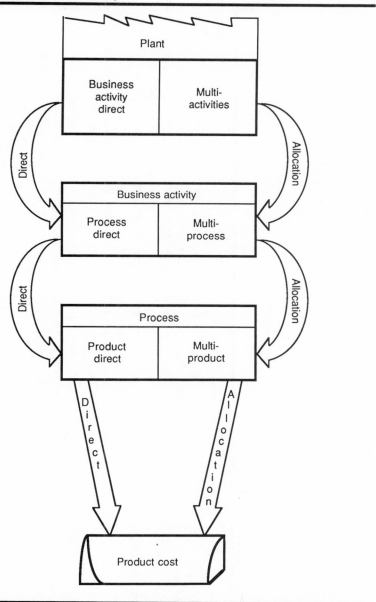

Table 4.2
Capital-Asset Categories

CATEGORY	DEFINITION
Factory equipment Process-specific	Factory equipment is used in the product-conversion process. Process-specific equipment includes machinery dedicated to performing a particular function in the manufacturing process. This may include a single machine, a group of like machines, or a group of different machines organized into a manufacturing cell.
Support equipment	Factory support equipment includes items that are not associated with a particular function within the manufacturing process. Material-handling equipment, which is used to transport parts and tools between different machines, machine groups, or cells, is an example of factory support equipment.
Business computer hardware/software	Business computer hardware and software is defined as the data-processing installation that handles the general business needs of the factory. The services of this installation apply to all functions of the organization and are not peculiar to a single process or product.
Function-specific computer hardware/software General-application	The general-application category is dedicated to the overall manufacturing process but not to particular machines, machine groups, or cells. It includes such items as a factory process-control computer installation.

Specific-application	Function-specific computer hardware and software with specific applications includes processors and software dedicated to a particular machine, machine group, or cell. An example of specific-application hardware is a microprocessor used to control a flexible machining cell. Specific-application software includes operating programs for running a machine and numerical control programs for processing particular parts.
Special tooling and test equipment	Special tooling and test equipment includes tools, dies, jigs, fixtures, gauges, and electronic equipment used for completing individual operations within the manufacturing process.
Startup costs Facility	Facility startup includes testing of the various systems and processes that are not peculiar to a machine, machine group, or cell prior to commencing any production in the facility. This includes tryout and debugging of continuous-process monitoring systems and material-handling systems.
Process	Process startup includes testing the individual machines, machine groups, or cells prior to commencing production. This includes tool tryout, process tryout, and debugging.

Source: James A. Brimson, and Leonard D. Frescoln, "Technology Accounting: The Value-Added Approach to Capital-Asset Depreciation," CIM Review (Fall 1986), 47.

Technology costs can be accumulated by the actual or standard costs, or both, which have been directly identified to the end user by a direct charge. For example, an industrial engineering project to improve material flow through a Group Technology cell could be charged directly to the cell. Or actual or standard costs can be initially charged to the business activity associated with the technology and then allocated to the process on some equitable basis. For example, industrial engineering business activity could be allocated to processes on a surrogate basis, such as square footage or capitalization. Whether a company allocates a business activity to processes by specific identification or on a surrogate basis depends upon the answers to two questions: Are the tasks performed by the business activity controlled by the users? and Is the administrative cost to identify services to users justified? If the business activity performs tasks specifically identified with the various processes, such as the material-flow study mentioned earlier, the process benefited theoretically should pay for that service directly. If specific identification of an activity requires extensive labor-charging on employee time records, the effort required to assign those costs accurately to the user processes may be disproportionate to the benefits derived from the information. In such cases, a surrogate allocation basis may provide a reasonable approximation of the causal/beneficial relation.

Examples of other business-activity allocations are material-handling equipment or systems, factory process-control systems, and facility-level startup costs. Many technology costs formerly accumulated in plantwide cost pools and allocated as overhead can be associated directly with specific engineering or manufacturing business-activity cost centers. The process-level technologies include the machine, machine group, or cell. Hence, they generally can be assigned directly to products on an actual usage basis. These costs should be accumulated by homogeneous groupings in accordance with the organization of the factory:

- Group Technology. When a process constitutes a cell with dissimilar equipment that can be thought of as a single manufacturing process, costs should be accumulated and allocated for the entire cell. Typically, the machines in the cell are functionally dissimilar (e.g., lathes, drills, and material-handling machines), so that parts can move through the entire manufacturing cycle in one location.

- A family of similar machines. When a manufacturing process is organized by groupings of machines that perform a unique function, a uniform rate can be calculated and charged for the entire machine group (e.g., lathes and drill mills). Costs of equipment are accounted for by machine but are accumulated and allocated to production for the entire group.
- In some cases, a single machine that represents a significant cost and that is unique in its function may constitute a machine group.

Determining cost centers, or the proper groupings for accumulating and allocating process costs depends upon the nature of the manufacturing process. A single-process facility such as a foundry may not require any breakdown of costs below the plant level, while a multiple-process facility that includes machinery, forming, and assembly functions may require a cost breakdown by process.

Does the plant produce a single product, multiple products with a high degree of commonality, or multiple products that are significantly different? There may be little need to segregate manufacturing costs into unique cost centers by cell or machine groups if the output of the plant is a single product. In this case, the traditional plantwide pool might suffice. If the plant produces significantly different products, the contribution of the several processes may vary significantly among the products. For example, one product may have a high concentration of precision-machined parts and relatively simple assembly while another product may have numerous sheet-metal parts and a very complex assembly process. In such cases, costs should be accumulated and allocated at the process level.

If a multiple-process facility produces large quantities of spare components in addition to end-item production, a breakdown of costs by process may be desirable to identify properly the costs of spare components.

If a multiple-function facility is subject to frequent make/buy adjustments, a breakdown of costs by process may be desirable in determining the true economics of the make/buy comparison.

Is manufacturing technology stable or subject to frequent change? Evaluation of the economics of technology alternatives may be assisted by segregating costs by process.

Some technology costs are assignable to specific products without being assigned to a process. Examples are numerical control

Table 4.3

TECHNOLOGY CATEGORY	RECOMMENDED ALLOCATION LEVEL
Factory equipment	
Process-specific	Product
Support	Process
Business computer	
hardware/software	Corporation or plant
Function-specific computer	
hardware/software	
General-application	Activity
Specific-application	Process
Specific tooling and	
test equipment	Product
Startup costs	
Facility	Activity
Process	Process

programs for specific parts and special tools, dies, jigs, fixtures, and gauges. Recommended allocation levels for the various categories of assets are shown in Table 4.3.

Computing the Technology Cost Basis

The second major step in determining value added is to calculate the technology cost basis. Capital equipment used in manufacturing processes traditionally has been charged to an operation on a historical cost basis. The cost of the equipment is recorded in a capital-equipment asset account, and that cost in turn is allocated to the appropriate cost pool in the form of a fixed-time depreciation charge. Typically, this cost has been treated as a fixed charge and has not represented a significant portion of total product costs.

In the modern manufacturing environment processes are becoming far more capital-intensive, and technological evolution is shortening the useful life of equipment. These factors combine to make capital-equipment investments a principal driver in the economics of manufacturing. With technology creating a greater turnover of equipment, factors such as interest costs, decline in value of equipment due to obsolescence, and cost to replace equipment must be included in product cost allocations to properly reflect the economic price in the marketplace. Traditional accounting systems in the United States have not treated these elements as components of product cost but rather as part of corporate general and administrative expenses.

Asset Cost. The asset cost is calculated as

$$\text{Purchase price} + \text{Startup cost} + \text{Current-cost adjustment}$$
$$+ \text{Interest} - \text{Residual value}$$

Current-Cost Adjustment. The concept of current cost implies a market value, which is independent of the purchase price of the asset. The market value represents the current price any company would pay to acquire a new, but similar, asset. This adjustment is added to the purchase price and startup cost to determine the updated depreciation allocation. Under the technology-accounting methodology, the value added by the technology can best be represented by the market value. Also, the inclusion of the intrinsic market value will result in the pricing mechanism creating sufficient revenue from product sales to fund the eventual replacement of the equipment. If pricing decisions are restricted to depreciation based on historical cost, it is likely that insufficient revenue will be generated to replace equipment in an inflationary or technologically changing environment. The current-cost adjustment provides for proper consideration of the real economics.

Interest. The acquisition of technology involves the acquisition of a capital asset. Since the asset is acquired prior to generating revenue, it must be acquired either through use of funds supplied from corporate capital or by borrowing. In either case, interest cost is incurred on the funds and should be considered when evaluating the economics of the acquisition.

The interest rate applied to the acquisition should represent the rate available to the corporation in the funds market for a similar class of assets. The rate may vary among different capital projects, both because of timing and the degree of risk involved in the project. It is critical to include this cost regardless of whether a company borrows funds externally. This method creates a reserve of funds, which not only offsets actual interest expense but also increases the retained earnings of the shareholders. The major capital assets in use should be evaluated annually to update the estimates of current cost and interest costs as well as the estimated service life over which such costs are to be allocated.

Asset Service Life. The rate at which the cost of the technology is assigned to a product depends on the assumed life of the asset or the projected production volume, or both. Two important factors contributing to asset life are physical life, the decline in performance of the asset due to wear and tear; and functional life, the obsolescence of an asset through technological change. An asset can become obsolete when demand for the product changes and the asset has no future economic value because it is peculiar to the product. An asset also can become obsolete if its impact on cost per unit of output is greater than allowed by the competitive marketplace.

The service life established for allocation of costs will normally be the functional life, because it represents the period of usefulness to the manufacturer and is typically shorter than the physical life for high-technology equipment. Computers, whose physical life is quite long, are generally replaced with newer equipment at frequent intervals. Thus, the functional life of the computer becomes the service life over which costs must be realized.

The original service life represents the estimated asset life at the time of acquisition. The asset life can be stated in terms of either a fixed time or a production volume (such as production units or machine hours). As noted earlier, a periodic re-evaluation of assets is necessary to update the various cost factors, including estimated service life. This process involves reviewing the original service-life estimate to determine if it is still reasonable.

The revised service life represents the impact of revised economic projections subsequent to acquisition. An extended service life normally provides a larger base upon which to recover the asset cost, while a shortened service life will reduce the recovery base and adversely affect product cost. Upgrades and refurbishments should be treated under this category.

Revisions to asset-life estimation normally occur for several reasons: (1) The asset becomes obsolete, physically or functionally, at a different rate than was forecast. (2) Demand is significantly different than was forecast, requiring changes in production volume. (3)

Table 4.4

CATEGORY	FIXED-TIME	VALUE-ADDED
Factory equipment		
Process-specific		x
Support		x
Business computer hardware/software	x	
Function-specific hardware/software		
General-application	x	
Specific-application		x
Special tooling and test equipment		x
Startup costs		
Facility	x	
Process		x

Source: James A. Brimson and Leonard D. Frescoln, "Technology Accounting: The Value-Added Approach to Capital-Asset Depreciation," CIM Review *(Fall 1986), 50.*

Stabilization or stagnation of technology typically extend service life, but advances in technology shorten service life.

The level of cost accumulation and allocation should govern the decision to use fixed-time or value-added methods for service lives. Assets that are assignable to a specific process should use a value-added approach, while assets assignable at the business activity or higher levels should use a fixed-time approach. The asset categories are listed in Table 4.4, with an indication of whether a fixed-time depreciation method or a value-added method is recommended.

As emphasized throughout this chapter, a capital asset's performance should be re-evaluated periodically to achieve proper matching of technology cost to products. This ensures that the value added by technology continues to be assigned to products past the original service life if the asset continues in production. Most current accounting systems do not provide for adjustment of service lives to allocate costs properly in case service-life estimates change.

Assignment Methodologies

Within the categories of fixed-time depreciation and value-added depreciation are several methods appropriate for specific circumstances.

Fixed-Time Depreciation Methods. The *straight-line method* is used when no major variations in demand are expected and when age, usage, or performance are not expected to result in significant increases to maintenance and repair costs over time. This method is most appropriate for buildings, furniture, computer hardware and software, and facility startup costs.

The *sum-of-the-years' digits method* is used when no major variations in demand are expected but a steady decline in performance of the asset is expected to result in greater costs of repair and maintenance over time. A greater share of depreciation is recognized in early years, with smaller shares in later years to offset repair and maintenance costs, thus leveling the total cost over the useful life.

The *declining balance method* is an alternative to the sum-of-the-years' digits method. A more rapid decline of depreciation is effected in early years, with a more gradual decline in later years. This method, like the sum-of-the-years' digits, is not advisable in the flexible manufacturing environment, where changing demand may significantly affect utilization over time.

Value-Added Depreciation Methods. The *units-of-production method* is appropriate when usage is expected to vary over time and equipment is dedicated to a single product or nearly identical parts.

The *machine hours method* is also used in an environment of variable usage but can be applied when a variety of products or significantly different parts are processed through the equipment. In order to use this method, it is necessary to measure and record machine hours by job.

The *surrogate machine hours method* is the same as machine hours except that it is employed when machine hours cannot be measured and recorded by job. Engineered standards for processing time and volume are applied to output to determine value added.

The *apportionment method* is used for a technology where only output of the major piece of equipment is accounted for using one of the value-added methods already described. Peripheral equipment in the cell is apportioned from the major-equipment base in ratio to the capital investment.

The *inventory velocity method* is used when the primary measurement of manufacturing performance is process-throughput time. Process throughput, rather than time on a machine, becomes the basis for allocating costs.

Accounting for Cost of Ownership. The following projection in Table 4.5 represents the estimate of costs of ownership for an asset and its corresponding allocation to production units at the time of acquisition.

Assume that at the end of the first year the production schedule of 250,000 units has been met but that new equipment is now available to meet an existing demand for 300,000 units per year. The pertinent facts and accompanying analysis of the proposed replacement (see Table 4.6) are as follows: In this case, replacement of the existing equipment with improved equipment results in greater unit production costs when all elements of the transaction are considered. Had the economic impact of disposition of the old equipment on the replacement not been considered, a cost benefit would have been perceived. Using this analysis, further alternatives may be explored. For example, another unit identical to the original one may be acquired for a market value of $400,000, thus providing the desired capacity plus some added margin at a reduced cost.

The replacement decision must also take into account technical factors, which could dictate a decision that increases costs in the short run but that provides a more effective long-term solution. For

Table 4.5
An Analysis of Costs of Ownership

Acquisition cost	$1,000,000
Estimated service life	1,000,000 units
Production rate	250,000 units/year
Current-cost factor	6% per year increase
Financing cost	9.5% on average book value (historical)

ELEMENT	YEAR 1	YEAR 2	YEAR 3	YEAR 4	TOTAL
Depreciation	$250,000	$250,000	$250,000	$250,000	$1,000,000
Current-cost adjustment	15,000	46,800	81,462	119,215	262,477
Interest	83,125	59,375	35,625	11,875	190,000
Total	$348,125	$356,175	$367,087	$381,090	$1,452,477
Total units					1,000,000
Cost/unit					$ 1.4525

Source: James A. Brimson and Leonard D. Frescoln, "Technology Accounting: The Value-Added Approach to Capital-Asset Depreciation," CIM Review *(Fall 1986), 52.*

Table 4.6
Analysis of Proposed Replacement

Acquisition cost of replacement	$1,000,000
Estimated service life	1,200,000 units
Production rate	300,000 units/year
Market value of current equipment	$400,000
Loss on disposition of old equipment	$335,000
Total cost of replacement (acquisition cost + loss)	$1,355,000
Current-cost factor	6% annual increase
Financing cost	9.5% on average book value (historical)

ELEMENT	YEAR 1	YEAR 2	YEAR 3	YEAR 4	YEAR 5	TOTAL
Depreciation	$250,000	$250,000	$250,000	$250,000	$250,000	$1,250,000
Current cost	15,000	15,000	48,800	81,462	119,215	277,477
Interest	83,125	83,125	59,375	35,625	11,875	273,125
Replacement loss		335,000				335,000
Total cost	$348,125	$683,125	$356,175	$367,087	$381,090	$2,135,602
Total units						1,450,000
Unit cost						$ 1.4728

Source: James A. Brimson and Leonard D. Frescoln, "Technology Accounting: The Value-Added Approach to Capital-Asset Depreciation," CIM Review (Fall 1986), 52.

example, the new equipment may be more flexible in adapting to possible future product variations. Thus, it may be a better long-term alternative at a relatively minor current cost.

Summary

The concept of technology accounting presented here necessitates several changes in traditional accounting practices employed by most manufacturers:

- A more direct method of matching technology costs to products (a departure from the traditional approach of using a direct-labor base and a plant overhead pool)
- Introducing economic factors to production costing in addition to the limited traditional elements of material, labor, and overhead
- Using key manufacturing measurements rather than financial measurements as the basis for allocating costs
- Increasing the utilization of value-added depreciation methods
- Integrating the concept of periodic economic re-evaluation into the cost accounting system

Technology accounting provides the economic-planning and decision-making base that has long been absent from cost accounting.

INTERNAL-CONTROL CONSIDERATIONS

Cost-effective approaches for internal controls should be developed as a company automates. An appropriate system of internal controls is fundamental to any accounting system. Without adequate controls, a manufacturer risks producing erroneous financial information. While the internal-control system will be significantly different in automated and manual environments, the following objectives apply to any type of transaction or account.

Authorization

Transactions must be authorized in conformance with management intent. Authorization procedures may be general, applying to a large number of similar transactions, or they may be specific. Policies establish general authorizations but often require specific authorizations for certain transactions. Typically, these transactions are nonrecurring and involve significant expenditure or risk, such as investments in technology.

Recording

All authorized transactions should be recorded at the correct amounts, in the accounting period in which they were executed, and in the appropriate accounting records. The physical evidence of recording includes documents (invoices, warehouse transfers) and records (subsidiary ledgers, general ledgers), in which the transactions are entered and summarized. Documents and records should be designed to lessen the possibility that a transaction will be recorded incorrectly, recorded more than once, or omitted.

Safeguarding

Responsibility for physical custody of assets is assigned to specific personnel, independent of related record-keeping functions. Both direct (physical) and indirect (paperwork) access to assets are limited to properly authorized personnel. Safeguarding is also achieved through physical precautions (for example, locking areas of the warehouse where high-value products are stored).

Reconciliation

Records are compared with physical assets, documents, or control accounts, such as periodic physical inventory. The nature and amount of any differences are determined, and appropriate adjustments are recorded. Reconciliation procedures help provide assurance that other control objectives have been achieved.

Valuation

Recorded amounts are reviewed for discrepancies in value. Direct write-downs, allowances, or other adjustments are made to conform to Generally Accepted Accounting Principles. This is especially true with obsolete or dated inventory.

As companies progress toward the goal of optimized manufacturing, internal control as practiced today will change because of the need to eliminate nonproductive costs and to minimize total lead time. Paper flow will be eliminated where possible and otherwise streamlined to reduce timing constraints and associated processing costs. The number of people who provide the typical "segregation of duties" may be reduced drastically. As a result, internal-control guidelines will need modification and review.

The move toward a paperless environment will have a significant impact on data-processing systems and policies. Documents so familiar to accountants and auditors may no longer exist; they would be replaced by computer transactions documenting the occurrence of an event. The typical approach of auditing around an EDP application may no longer suffice—auditing the "black box" itself will be required. The application of expert systems will pose a special problem for auditors; results may not always duplicate, because of the learning abilities of a system. Heuristic expert systems can select different paths from input to output, depending on the input, the output, and the state of many other variables. Therefore, true audits of such systems would require tracing from input to output for each transaction, given the state of all measured variables at the time the transaction was made—a feat that generally would be impossible to guarantee.

Transactions probably will originate in different areas within an organization. Authorization, processing, and associated accounting entries will be modified to reflect changes in the manufacturing environment, management philosophies, and the organizational structure. Internal-control procedures must provide the cost-effective checks and balances needed for good management practices. Creative approaches will be required.

CMS CASE STUDIES

To illustrate alternative cost accounting methods in a typical factory, a model has been created to provide a database for testing various situations.[3] The model consists of operating data for all departments of a small (hypothetical) manufacturing company called the CAM-I Company. The company is a durable-goods manufacturer with three product lines in current production. In

---

3. This model was developed by Leonard D. Frescoln and John K. Mulligan, Williams International.

addition, it produces spare parts for its products in the field, which account for approximately 10 percent of annual volume, and it performs R&D work under contract, accounting for approximately 12 percent of annual volume.

The company's products are all high-cost, low-volume items. Approximately one-half of product cost is related to purchased parts and subcontracted items. The other half is related to manufactured parts and assembly operations. The company manufactures machined parts; performs sheet-metal fabrication, component assembly, and final assembly; and tests operations. Tooling for parts manufactured in-house and for assembly operations is fabricated in a tool shop, which doubles as an experimental manufacturing center for R&D items.

The company has 585 employees, occupies 123,000 sq. ft., and has annual sales of $60 million. Total cost of operation is $53.1 million. The company is divided into four major organizations. The operating organizations are subdivided into twenty-nine cost centers for cost collection and allocation purposes. We have concentrated on the manufacturing cost centers for purposes of this model. The engineering organization has not been broken down to lower levels. A table accompanies each case, detailing all pertinent information included in the database. The tables identify cost center numbers, cost center descriptions, staffing, square footage, capital equipment, cost-allocation bases, and labor rates. In addition, information on depreciation methods, insurance rates, tax rates, product-line allocation, and price is given.

Case 1

There are four indirect cost pools: manufacturing, engineering, material handling, and general and administrative (G&A). The manufacturing and engineering pools use a direct labor-dollar basis for allocating indirect costs, material-handling indirect costs are allocated on a direct-material basis, and general and administrative expenses are allocated on total cost input (inventory cost). (See Table 4.7.)

Case 2

The manufacturing operation is subdivided into seven pools: machine shop, sheet metal, heat-treating, assembly and testing, manu-

Table 4.7
Case 1. Four Pools, Multiple Allocation Bases

	PRODUCTS			SPARES	R&D	TOTAL
	A	B	C			
Direct labor	$ 3,373	$ 2,230	$1,559	$1,111	$ 551	$ 8,824
Manufacturing overhead	4,249	2,810	1,964	1,399	695	11,117
Direct material	7,000	8,000	3,000	1,000	1,000	20,000
Material handling	549	627	235	79	79	1,569
Engineering labor	479	288	192	96	1,840	2,895
Engineering overhead	681	408	272	136	2,614	4,111
Total manufacturing cost	$16,331	$14,363	$7,222	$3,821	$6,779	$48,516
G&A	1,559	1,372	690	365	647	4,633
Total product cost	$17,890	$15,735	$7,912	$4,186	$7,426	$53,149

Source: Leonard D. Frescoln and John K. Mulligan, Williams International.

facturing engineering, quality assurance, and product support. All seven pools use a direct labor-dollar allocation basis. The material-control cost centers (inventory and production control), which were included in the plantwide manufacturing pool in case 1, have been allocated to the seven process pools on a direct labor-hour basis. All other indirect cost allocations remain unchanged from case 1. (See Table 4.8.)

Case 3

The manufacturing operation is subdivided into fifteen pools by further dividing the machine shop, sheet metal, and assembly and test departments into separate pools for each cost center at the lowest organizational level. These new process pools are lathes, mills, grinding, drills, stamping, forming, welding, subassembly, final assembly, paint shop, and production testing. The allocation basis for all these pools remains direct-labor dollars. All other pools are unchanged from case 2. (See Table 4.9.)

Case 4

This case assumes that the CAM-I Company has made a decision to automate the lathe and mill cost centers as a first step toward computer-integrated manufacturing. The company replaces sixteen of its eighteen conventional lathes, ten CNC lathes, and two CNC machining centers. This modernization effort results in a capital investment of $3.8 million for the lathe cost center, up from $1 million in conventional equipment, but allows for a reduction in staff from forty people on two shifts to twenty-one people on two shifts. The reduction is made possible by the ability of one operator to run two machines in the CNC environment. (See Table 4.10.)

The parallel project in the milling cost center increases capital investment from $1.6 million to $4.3 million and reduces the staff from thirty-five people to eighteen. In this cost center 14 of the 116 conventional mills were replaced with ten CNC mills and two CNC five-axis mills. As a result of this transformation, it became evident that product cost is more sensitive to the employment of capital than to labor. Furthermore, with one operator on two machines, allocation of operator labor to jobs would be difficult.

Table 4.8
Case 2. Seven Pools, Direct-Labor Allocation Basis

	PRODUCTS			SPARES	R&D	TOTAL
	A	B	C			
Direct labor	$ 3,373	$ 2,230	$1,559	$1,111	$ 551	$ 8,824
Manufacturing overhead	4,218	2,614	1,912	1,733	640	11,117
Direct material	7,000	8,000	3,000	1,000	1,000	20,000
Material handling	549	627	235	79	79	1,569
Engineering labor	479	288	192	96	1,840	2,895
Engineering overhead	681	408	272	136	2,614	4,111
Total manufacturing cost	$16,300	$14,167	$7,170	$4,155	$6,724	$48,516
G&A	1,556	1,353	685	397	642	4,633
Total product cost	$17,856	$15,520	$7,855	$4,552	$7,366	$53,149

Source: Leonard D. Frescoln and John K. Mulligan, Williams International.

Table 4.9
Case 3. Fifteen Pools, Direct-Labor Allocation Basis

| | PRODUCTS | | | | | |
	A	B	C	SPARES	R&D	TOTAL
Direct manufacturing	$ 3,373	$ 2,230	$1,559	$1,111	$ 551	$ 8,824
Manufacturing overhead	4,237	2,611	1,898	1,731	640	11,117
Direct material	7,000	8,000	3,000	1,000	1,000	20,000
Material handling	549	627	235	79	79	1,569
Engineering labor	479	288	192	96	1,840	2,895
Engineering overhead	681	408	272	136	2,614	4,111
Total manufacturing cost	$16,319	$14,164	$7,156	$4,153	$6,724	$48,516
G&A	1,558	1,353	683	397	642	4,633
Total product cost	$17,877	$15,517	$7,839	$4,550	$7,366	$53,149

Source: Leonard D. Frescoln and John K. Mulligan, Williams International.

128

Table 4.10
Case 4. Introduction of Machine-Hours Allocation Basis

	PRODUCTS			SPARES	R&D	TOTAL
	A	B	C			
Direct manufacturing	$ 4,000	$ 2,701	$1,996	$1,353	$ 551	$10,601
Manufacturing overhead	2,921	2,123	1,333	1,614	627	8,618
Direct material	7,000	8,000	3,000	1,000	1,000	20,000
Material handling	549	627	235	79	79	1,569
Engineering labor	479	288	192	96	1,840	2,895
Engineering overhead	681	408	272	136	2,614	4,111
Total manufacturing cost	$15,630	$14,147	$7,028	$4,278	$6,711	$47,794
G&A	1,515	1,371	681	415	651	4,633
Total product cost	$17,145	$15,518	$7,709	$4,693	$7,362	$52,427

Source: Leonard D. Frescoln and John K. Mulligan, Williams International.

Therefore, the decision was made to allocate costs to production on a machine-hour basis in these two cost centers.

Conversion of cost centers 1101 and 1102 to automated equipment reduced total cost of operations by $721,400. However, savings were not realized on all product lines, when product cost allocation is compared with case 3. Product A realized a significant cost reduction. Product B remained unchanged. Product C realized a modest reduction. Spares costs increased. This resulted from significant differences in application of machine hours among the products when compared with application of labor hours under conventional methods.

Case 5

This case assumes the CAM-I Company has moved toward manufacturing simplification by reorganizing the plant into a Group Technology—oriented process. (See Table 4.11.)

The company rearranged the sheet-metal shop into two complete cells: one to handle large sheet stock and the other to handle small stock. All stamping and forming operations are conducted in these two cells, based on the size of the stock, from which a part is made. The welding area remains a unique operation and services all cells, regardless of the part.

The machine shop, which includes all lathes, mills, grinders, and drills, was rearranged into five cellular manufacturing process areas. The cells were arranged as follows:

1. The prismatic cell, for chucked and odd-shaped parts
2. Round bar stock cell
3. The primary machining cell
4. Secondary machining cell
5. Finish machining cell

Cells were arranged so that a part or raw material flows in one door, is processed in a "horse-shoe" process line, and is completed and sent out another door. The part is then expedited either to another cell for further machining or to WIP stores until it is ready for subassembly or final assembly. Each cell was designed to complete as much of the manufacturing process on the part as possible (with the exception of heat-treating and welding). The plant was rearranged so that the flow of all parts follows a specific path that leads

Table 4.11
Case 5. Cell-Time Allocation Basis

	PRODUCTS			SPARES	R&D	TOTAL
	A	B	C			
Direct manufacturing	$ 4,101	$ 3,111	$2,015	$1,473	$ 551	$11,251
Manufacturing overhead	2,263	1,939	1,041	1,411	627	7,281
Direct material	7,000	8,000	3,000	1,000	1,000	20,000
Material handling	549	628	235	79	79	1,570
Engineering labor	479	288	192	96	1,840	2,895
Engineering overhead	682	409	273	136	2,619	4,119
Total manufacturing cost	$15,074	$14,375	$6,756	$4,195	$6,716	$47,116
G&A	1,457	1,389	653	405	649	4,553
Total product cost	$16,531	$15,764	$7,409	$4,600	$7,365	$51,669

Source: Leonard D. Frescoln and John K. Mulligan, Williams International.

from receiving to shipping with as little backward movement as possible. This is another step toward a computer-integrated manufacturing facility.

Case 5 incorporates the new automatic CNC equipment purchased in case 4 for the lathe and milling operations. An additional reduction of six people was made possible in this case because of the added ability of one worker to run multiple pieces of equipment. In addition, the stamping and forming equipment was replaced or upgraded, or both, to incorporate the cellular process applications. This resulted in capital expenditures of $4 million but allowed for a reduction in staff of six people. The welding area was kept as an autonomous area because of the need to service all the manufacturing cells. To improve work flow in this area, robotic technology was introduced at a cost of $650,000 in capital expenditures. This technology made possible a reduction of five people in the welding area.

With the conversion of the manufacturing operations to cellular processing, the sensitivity of product cost to capital investment rather than to labor was further reinforced. Worker reductions resulting from one person running multiple machines made allocation of cost based on operator labor difficult. For this reason, costs were allocated to production based on cell time in the process operations.

Since direct charges for each cell are based on the actual time each product line occupies the cell, there are no longer any direct-labor charges in the process operations. Time is monitored as a fallout of the manufacturing control system. For this reason, two timekeepers were eliminated from the finance department.

This type of environment has allowed the CAM-I Company to reduce the manufacturing lead time by 25 percent. The reduced lead time, together with a $750,000 cost reduction, allowed CAM-I to reduce the amount of capital invested in inventory by 29 percent, a cost that was passed on to the customers, thereby improving the competitive position of the company. To allow a direct comparison to the other cases, we have assumed that no price reductions were passed on to customers and no additional volume was undertaken.

Case 6

This case assumes that the CAM-I Company has decided to automate the manufacturing environment in case 5 to computer-integrated manufacturing in the sheet-metal and machining areas. The company installed automated guided vehicles in the shop area to expedite parts and tools between receiving, the process operations, the tool shop, and WIP stores. The AGVs cost $1.1 million to install but allowed for the elimination of six workers in material control, who were no longer needed to track and expedite parts and material. (See Table 4.12.)

The company also installed an automated retrieval system in WIP stores at a cost of $1 million. This system automatically stores parts in various bins and staging areas until all lower-level parts and assemblies become available for subassembly or final assembly. The system then gathers parts when ready and queues the work for assembly.

Finally, a continuous-process monitoring system was installed in each of the process operation cells. This system provides immediate and accurate inspection of parts as they are made. It allows operators to make adjustments to equipment before several bad parts are detected. This system cost $100,000 per cell but reduced the quality assurance staff by eighteen inspectors and scrap rates by 50 percent. These lower scrap and rework rates also allowed a reduction of staff by five engineers, who formerly tracked and evaluated those parts.

All these systems are tied into a process-control computer (investment $2.1 million), which ensures smooth process flow. The computer automatically tracks all work at the part-level detail, including time on machine, time in cell, time in process, scrap rates, rework rates, and machine/cell downtime. The system provides cost data that helped reduce the staff in finance by two people, who were formerly required to compile such information manually. Because of all the reductions in staff, the personnel department was reduced by two people.

To support the new environment, two manufacturing engineers were added to monitor, control, and create process plans consistent with the system's requirements. Support for the process-control computer is provided by the existing staff in MIS.

The company invested $4.9 million in this stage of CIM conversion, resulting in net annual cost reductions of $803,000 and reduction of manufacturing lead times to 25 percent of the lead times in cases 1–4. The reduction in the manufacturing lead time also helped reduce the finished-goods inventory by 75 percent. The reduced lead time and reductions in cost allowed the CAM-I Com-

Table 4.12
Case 6. CIM Environment

	PRODUCTS			SPARES	R&D	TOTAL
	A	B	C			
Direct manufacturing	$ 4,184	$ 3,121	$2,082	$1,514	$ 550	$11,451
Manufacturing overhead	2,169	1,882	1,046	1,338	555	6,990
Direct material	7,000	8,000	3,000	1,000	1,000	20,000
Material handling	475	543	204	68	68	1,358
Engineering labor	450	268	182	92	1,720	2,712
Engineering overhead	663	395	268	135	2,532	3,993
Total manufacturing cost	$14,941	$14,209	$6,782	$4,147	$6,425	$46,504
G&A	1,402	1,333	636	389	603	4,363
Total product cost	$16,343	$15,542	$7,418	$4,536	$7,028	$50,867

Sources: Leonard D. Frescoln and John K. Mulligan, Williams International.

pany to reduce the amount of capital invested in inventories by 81 percent from case 5 and by 87 percent from case 4. This cost was passed on to the customers and affects the competitiveness of the company. For direct comparison to the other cases, we have assumed that no price reductions were passed on to customers and no additional volume was undertaken.

Comparison of Cases 1–6

Product/business-segment cost allocations for cases 1–6 are summarized in Table 4.13. The summary shows that, for the particular set of circumstances entered into the model for the CAM-I Company, the plantwide pool approach in case 1 tends to understate significantly the costs of spare parts, principally at the expense of products B and C. After developing pools for the major processes in case 2, the allocation to spares increases significantly, the allocation to product B decreases significantly, and the allocations to product A, product C, and R&D decrease slightly. The establishment of process pools by machine group in case 3 yields almost the same allocation as case 2. Allocation becomes somewhat different in case 4 as a result of equipment changes made to the lathe and milling cost centers, with significant reduction to product A, nominal reduction to product B, and a nominal increase to the spares/service product line because of its labor-intensity.

Incorporation of process operations in case 5 reduces the total cost of operations by $1,478,100 from case 3 and $756,700 from case 4. Again, these savings are not realized on all product lines,

Table 4.13
Case Study Summary

	PRODUCT					
	A	B	C	SPARES	R&D	TOTAL
Case 1	$17,891	$15,735	$7,911	$4,185	$7,426	$53,148
Case 2	17,856	15,521	7,855	4,550	7,366	53,148
Case 3	17,877	15,517	7,839	4,549	7,366	53,148
Case 4	17,146	15,518	7,710	4,692	7,361	52,427
Case 5	16,531	15,764	7,408	4,600	7,365	51,670
Case 6	16,344	15,542	7,418	4,536	7,027	50,867

when compared to prior cases. Products A and C realize a significant cost reduction, while product B shows a cost increase. Spares cost increases from cases 1–3 but decreases from case 4. The difference is attributable to the application of cell-occupancy time among the various product lines, when compared with application of labor hours under conventional methods. The CIM environment in case 6 again reduces the cost of operations by $846,000 from case 5, $1,560,000 from case 4, and $2,300,000 from cases 1–3. Product A continues to improve against all other cases. Product B realizes some improvement from cases 1 and 5 but shows no significant changes for cases 2–4. Product C shows almost no change from case 5 but does show some improvement from cases 1–4. Both spares and R&D show some improvement because of lower costs that resulted from capital improvements.

REFERENCES AND FURTHER READINGS

Abdel-khalik, A. R., and E. J. Lusk. "Transfer Pricing: A Synthesis." *The Accounting Review* (January 1974): 8–23.

Balachandran, B., and R. Ramakrishnan. "Joint Cost Allocation: A Unified Approach." *The Accounting Review* (January 1981): 85–96.

Bierman, H. "Inventory Valuation: The Use of Market Prices." *The Accounting Review* (October 1967): 731–737.

Billera, L. J., D. C. Heath, and R. E. Verrecchia. "A Unique Procedure for Allocating Common Costs from a Production Process." *Journal of Accounting Research* (Spring 1981): 185–196.

Callen, J. "Financial Cost Allocation: A Game Theoretic Approach." *The Accounting Review* (April 1978): 303–308.

Crosby, Phillip B. *Quality Is Free.* New York: McGraw-Hill, 1979.

Fine, Charles E. "Quality Control and Learning in Productive Systems." Working Paper, Graduate School of Business, Stanford University, January 1982.

Gordon, Cooper, Falk, and Miller. "The Pricing Decision." New York: National Association of Accountants and The Society of Management Accountants of Canada, 1982.

Hamlen, S. S., W. A. Hamlen, and J. T. Tschirhart. "The Use of the Generalized Shapley Allocation in Joint Cost Allocation." *The Accounting Review* (April 1980): 269–287.

————. "The Use of Core Theory in Evaluating Joint Cost-Allocation Schemes." *The Accounting Review* (July 1977): 616–627.

Jensen, D. L. "A Class of Mutually Satisfactory Allocations." *The Accounting Review* (October 1977): 842–856.

Juran, J. M. "Japanese and Western Quality—A Contract." *Quality Progress* (December 1978): 10–18.

Kaplan, R. S. "Measuring Manufacturing Performance: A New Challenge for Managerial Accounting Research." *The Accounting Review* (October 1983): 686–704.

Lemke, K. W. "In Defense of the 'Profit Center' Concept." *Abacus* (December 1970): 182–188.

Pinches, George E. "Myopia, Capital Budgeting, and Decision Making." *Financial Management* (Autumn 1982): 6–19.

Porter, M. E. *Competitive Strategy: Techniques for Analyzing Industries and Competitors.* New York: Free Press, 1980.

Richardson, P. R., and J. R. M. Gordon. "Measuring Total Manufacturing Performance." *Sloan Management Review* (Winter 1980): 47–58.

Roth, A., and R. E. Verrecchia. "The Shapley Value as Applied to Cost Allocation: A Reinterpretation." *The Journal of Accounting Research* (Spring 1979): 295–303.

Skinner, W. "The Focused Factory." *Harvard Business Review* (May–June 1974): 113–121.

Thomas, A. L. *A Behavioural Analysis of Joint Cost Allocation and Transfer Pricing.* Champaign, IL: Stipes, 1980.

Watson, D. J. H., and J. V. Baumier. "Transfer Pricing: A Behavioral Context." *The Accounting Review* (July 1975): 466–474.

Zimmerman, J. L. "The Costs and Benefits of Cost Allocation." *The Accounting Review* (July 1979): 504–521.

CHAPTER 5

Life-Cycle Management

L ife-cycle management focuses on those activities that occur prior to production to ensure the lowest total life-cycle cost. Because more than 90 percent of a product's cost is determined in preproduction phases, front-end planning is required to capitalize on opportunities for eliminating waste. Accounting emphasis should be expanded to include not only the production phase (where production costs are incurred) but also the design phase (where production costs are determined). Figure 5.1 illustrates the contrast between matched-cost or cash-flow concepts and the life-cycle concept.

Because the matched-cost and cash-flow curves rise sharply in production, traditional accounting is focused on this stage. Yet it is clear that life-cycle costs (the upper curve) have stabilized by the time production begins. Life-cycle management therefore dictates that the tightest controls be placed on the design phases, because costs are locked in after this point.

For the same reasons, CMS also focuses on the development phases of a product's life cycle. The system must provide information to enable engineering to make sound decisions in areas that have cost implications. Engineers currently are evaluated on their abilities to conform to form, fit, and function specifications. But it seems clear that engineers should also conform to cost specifications (design to cost).

Simply changing the cost accounting system, however, is not enough. Management philosophy must also change. Individuals should be rewarded for practices that minimize life-cycle cost. At present, rewards are given for good performance in single accounting periods or in organizational units. Manufacturers should develop new baselines that represent the lowest costs available, given the current state of the art in engineering and manufacturing. Baselines can be driven down by employing improved technologies.

Figure 5.1
Conflicts Between Current Accounting Practices and the Life-Cycle Concept

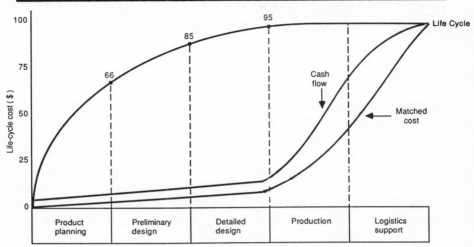

Source: Adapted from Benjamin S. Blanchard, Design and Manage to Life-Cycle Cost. Portland, OR: M/A Press, 1978.

LIFE-CYCLE COSTING AND REPORTING

In the past, much cost accounting emphasis had been placed on physical production (recurring costs). The CMS Conceptual Design model focuses on a broader range of costs, including the nonrecurring costs that arise during the product-development and product logistics support phases of a product's life cycle. Visibility of these costs becomes increasingly important as companies implement life-cycle planning for new products or for existing product lines.

Studies show that about 90 percent of a product's life-cycle cost is determined by decisions made early in the cycle (see Figure 5.2). In many industries automation shifts the basis of competition to product and process development, thereby requiring substantial investments. The practice of treating product- and process-development activities as period operating expenses should be altered; the long-term impact on a firm's total cost structure suggests, rather, that major activities should be viewed as capital investments and ultimately charged to products that benefit from these investments.

Figure 5.2
Total Life-Cycle Cost Profile

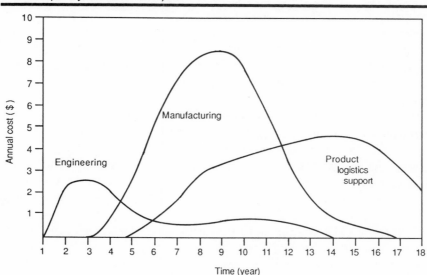

Source: Richard Engwall, Westinghouse Electric Corporation.

Life-cycle costing is necessary to provide a better picture of long-term product profitability; to show the effectiveness of life-cycle planning; to quantify the cost impact of alternatives chosen during the engineering design phase; and to assign the costs of technology to products that use the technology.

Product costs that arise during the development, production, and product logistics support phases must be linked to provide a long-term profitability picture and to support key management decisions about product line, mix, and pricing. This becomes critical in environments where product life cycles are short (or shrinking), because prices ultimately must recover all costs plus profit (adequate return on capital invested).

The CMS Engineering/Manufacturing Functional Model serves as the basis for reporting product life-cycle costs. Cost data will be accumulated across multiple years by product, function, activity, and cost element. Accounting-period expenses (such as product development, marketing, and distribution costs) must be assigned directly to a product or allocated using an appropriate basis. This ensures that these costs will be included in pricing and profit decisions.

Variances from standard could be recorded at the process instead of the product level. The detailed level of control would be more appropriate in low-volume or custom manufacturing environments, or in high-volume environments with a varied mix of products.

Nonrecurring costs arising during the development and product logistics support phases would be accumulated during the course of a project. Upon completion of the project, the data could be transferred to a historical database to support planning. The amount of data transferred (detail versus summary) would be based on requirements to support budgeting, life-cycle planning, and parametric estimation of future projects.

Process R&D becomes an important consideration in technology-intensive environments, since large investments may be involved and numerous product lines may benefit. As technologies emerge from R&D, CMS must accurately charge the full cost of the technology to benefiting products. This could be done by establishing a project cost accumulation system to capture actual costs at the planned level of detail. When the project is done, the technology cost would be charged to the manufacturing process and then assigned to products, using the approach suggested in the Technology Accounting section of Chapter 4.

NONRECURRING COSTS—PROJECT ACCOUNTING AND CONTROL

Traditional cost accounting systems have focused primarily on recurring conversion costs. CMS must add information on strategically important nonrecurring costs, thus providing a mechanism for controlling significant long-term investments and supporting future planning. Examples of strategic projects could include major programs for product and process R&D, quality improvement, or worker training. These projects often last more than a year and are included in the capital budget. They affect many departments and activities within the facility and may require different levels of involvement from a single organizational unit at different times.

Accounting treatment of the cost (capitalize versus expense) will be based on the type of project and on company policy.

CMS must have project reporting capabilities for progress reporting and control. As with any major expenditure or project, costs must be collected, compared to budgeted amounts, and reported for multiple years. Different levels of cost detail may be desired, based on the complexity of the project, management's need for information, and the potential uses of the historical information for budgeting and planning future projects. CMS would support standard project-reporting features like descriptive and budget information; summary and detail reporting for individual or specific types of projects; accumulation of totals for the current accounting period, year-to-date, and inception-to-date (across multiple years); and the ability to archive closed projects to a historical database for future analysis and planning.

THE ROLE OF THE MANAGEMENT ACCOUNTANT

Management accounting techniques should be a part of the product review process. To date, management accountants have focused on the maturity and decline of a product's life cycle. More participation is needed in the startup and growth stages. Table 5.1 shows how the stages of a product's life cycle and management's information needs are related.

Key areas where management accounting involvement can be most effective are business and competitor modeling, product costs, investment proposal, project control, abandonment analysis, and whole-life cost considerations. Many of the traditional activities of the management accountant will be replaced by computer systems. The accountant's role will be to participate actively in the design, implementation, control, and analysis of these systems.

PRODUCT COSTS

This section presents the requirements and problems associated with the establishment of product costs. The task is to calculate or estimate accurately the cost of a new product and to track movement in costs throughout the product life cycle. This cost must be monitored and compared to the target cost determined by the strategic plan and market evaluation. Integrating the corporate

Table 5.1
Total Life-Cycle Cost Profile

STAGE	FACTORS	MANAGEMENT ACCOUNTING INFLUENCE		
		NOW	TOOLS NEEDED	INFORMATION
1. Corporate structure Business/Planning strategy		Low Low	Provision of basic financial model	ROI ROAM Growth Interprets corporate plan Connecting link
2. Market evaluation	Market position Competition analysis Products Share Political/legislation Impact on existing product range Pricing/Exchange rates Go/No go	Low	Competitor analysis Basic model Comparison Market financial model	TAM SAM Growth Competitor analysis Market segmentation

3. Product response	Cost-of-sales target Project timing Volume Specification	Low	Product cost awareness Volume sensitivity Mat. price sensitivity Risks, opportunities	Technology available Manufacturing/design Margins needs Comp. product analysis
4. Investment proposal	Volume Price Development Capital investment Working capital Make/buy Lifetime Support costs Quality Spares Startup costs	Medium	Product cost Product P/L Balance sheet Sensitivity Risks, opportunities Cost of capital Waste	All normal accounting data plus all that identified in first three stages and flexible parameters

Figure 5.3
Position in Product Life-Cycle Model

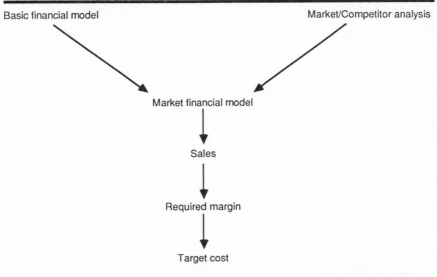

financial model with the market and competitor analysis produces a market and product financial model, which yields sales, margin, and target cost information. Figure 5.3 shows how the modeling effort fits into the product life-cycle model.

A sales estimator prepares the market and product financial model. Source data for the model come from each of the other business functions, such as engineering and manufacturing. Information must flow across functional lines and to and from sales estimating. Figure 5.4 indicates the cooperation required. The information required includes engineering design status; engineering BOM (bill of material); volumes; volume-related labor, machine, and overhead rates; labor, machine, and overhead rates that reflect intended manufacturing method and rate movement; current and estimated movement in material cost over time; and planned cost reduction.

Contingency Costs

The estimator can use basic financial modeling software and what-if scenarios to obtain not only a projected product cost but also a

Figure 5.4
Areas of Influence

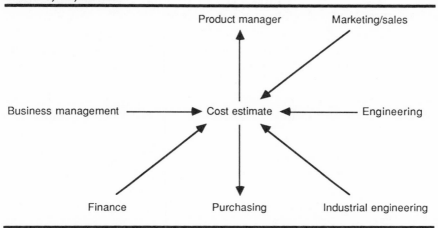

measure of risk. One way to do this is to consult with the product manager and other engineering and manufacturing managers to determine the degree of stability in the plan at various stages in the product life cycle. The managers can then assign a risk factor to each of the critical stages in the life-cycle model. The model should then convert the risk into cost impact. These costs, also, must appear in the product cost estimate.

Responsibilities of Other Functions
Accurate product costing depends on a number of inputs from various manufacturing functions.

Engineering contributes a stable engineering environment, accurate material requirements (BOM), cost awareness, understanding of manufacturing and testing capabilities, respect for quality, a knowledge of competitor methods, and definition and projection of cost reductions.

Industrial Engineering contributes information on method of manufacture, alternative techniques, future developments in manufacturing methods (JIT, CIM), and competitor methods.

Finance supplies labor- or machine-hour rates that reflect the proposed methods of manufacture; labor and overhead rates that reflect proposed volumes; a projection of inflation; cognizance of total portfolio costs and the impact of growth or decline of other products; apportionment of overhead; depreciation policy (particularly the assessment of assets life and the treatment of software); reassessment of fixed and variable overhead following consideration of manufacturing method; an indication of rate sensitivity; accurate information on the cost of fixed and working capital.

Purchasing contributes awareness of worldwide movement in component prices over time, volumes, "used on" status and quality of components, and total business purchasing power.

Marketing and Planning provides information on volumes and on target costs, including assessment of size and timing of cost reductions required to offset price erosion.

Business Management contributes sourcing, investment capital, and information on such nonfinancial considerations as geographical location and political and social consequences.

ORGANIZATIONAL STRUCTURE

The determination and control of life-cycle costs are the responsibility of the cost engineer. This section describes the cost engineer's role and relations with other manufacturing functions within a conventional project management organizational structure.

Cost engineering has evolved in response to an organizational need. Current accounting practices do not reflect accurate conversion costs when some processes are capital-intensive and others are not—a fact long recognized by cost estimators and others associated with make/buy decisions. Inadequate cost information can lead to less-than-optimal decisions. Cost engineering should be part of a manufacturer's organizational structure. Experience has shown that other reporting lines (e.g., commercial, engineering, or financial) limit cost engineering's effectiveness.

Proposal Stage

At the proposal stage (and throughout the product life cycle) the cost engineer estimates the significant cost elements and determines what they should cost. In short, the cost engineer determines the likely cost-of-sales, even though the project is still at the conceptual stage. Being part of the manufacturing organization enhances the cost engineer's credibility, since the job involves committing manufacturing to meet engineering targets. Thus, estimates of the financial viability of a proposal are determined largely by the cost engineer.

Design Phase

During the design phase the cost engineer's role is one of refinement and monitoring of the initial estimates. Target costs are decomposed through the bill of materials; cost drivers are identified. The objective is "design to cost," and here the cost engineer must work closely with purchasing to determine likely component costs, with production engineering to optimize manufacturing methods, and with quality assurance to match the product to the customer's expectations within the quoted price. During this phase the cost engineer should be located in the design office. Indeed, as a general principle, cost engineering should be located wherever the center of action is. Once a cost target is reached, further design work should stop and the effort should be directed elsewhere. The cost engineer's main tool is a set of computer programs that roll up the current-cost elements and add an allowance to give the unit production costs and the cost-of-sales. These figures and their trends are much valued by project management. The programs also list cost drivers and the progress toward attaining targets.

Production Phase

During the production phase the cost targets for manufactured items must be converted to target times for the shop floor. Good liaison with production engineering during the design phase to determine the best manufacturing methods facilitates this (though some modification doubtless will be required when processes are considered in detail). Similarly, allowances must be made for setup and learning. Actual times and costs must be monitored against targets, and significant deviations must be investigated. In practice, monitoring the cost elements will probably be sufficient. Thus, the cost engineer can determine remedial action when necessary, the cost to complete, and the cost at completion.

Cost engineers should have a background of engineering, production engineering, estimating, or some combination of these. A working knowledge of management accounting is essential. In effect, cost engineers combine the roles of estimating and cost accountancy using the computer aids to enhance their productivity.

INVESTMENT PROPOSAL

This section discusses the life-cycle cost factors to be considered once development of a product reaches the point where management must seek funds for its manufacture. An investment proposal has three goals: (1) to codify the investment justification, (2) to gain written approval, and (3) to specify the project's control base.

Management Accountant's Role

The management accountant must be involved in determining the product response, that is, must understand the product life-cycle cost *to the customer*. Figure 5.5 illustrates the trade-off between acquisition cost and operating and maintenance costs, as seen by the customer. It is also important for the accountant to understand the customer's perception of quality-versus-price in terms of the life-cycle cost. This helps the accountant evaluate the various product response options prior to formalizing the investment proposal.

At the investment proposal stage, the management accountant should do the following:

- Evaluate the proposal on a "total company" basis
- Assess the proposal's impact on the strategic plan
- Exercise "duty of care" to question all the assumptions
- Assess the sensitivity of the proposal to shifts in key parameters
- Assess key opportunities and risks; assist in developing a risk-management plan

Figure 5.5
Trade-off in Life-Cycle Costs to Customer

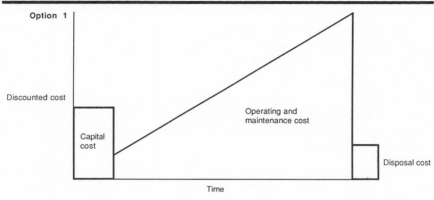

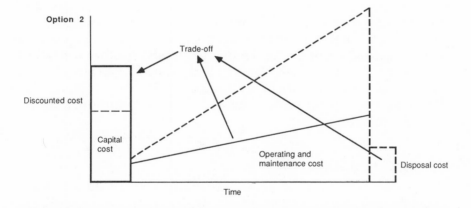

- Weight the main success factors
- Consider the synergy potential of opportunities such as the use of shared facilities
- Consider the impact of exchange-rate fluctuations and the costs of hedging
- Ensure that a manageable portfolio of products or product ranges, related to the strategic plan, is selected for life-cycle costing
- Ensure that long-term support costs (spares, warranty, updates) are considered

- Assist with the projection of launch costs (possibly using learning-curve theory) for both manufacturing and marketing (including warranty)
- Consider all available grants and taxation effects
- Ensure that weight is given to the intangible benefits
- Apply project-evaluation techniques, such as discounted cash flow (DCF), payback, and return-on-equity (ROE)
- Use personal experience to make allowances (plan contingencies) for items like engineering change notices
- Give due consideration to the effects of capital decay when evaluating the proposal

It also is necessary to maintain a dynamic modeling capability for evaluation sensitivities, what-if queries, and providing feedback for the strategic plan; to continually reassess the company's cost of capital and investment hurdle rates; and to organize the management accounting function so that someone is always in a position to provide a flexible response on all product issues. In the proposal itself, the management accountant must also adopt an approach to allocating and apportioning technology costs, overhead, fixed assets, and working capital. The approach should be consistent with cost accounting practices of the company. However, most cost accounting systems are not structured to provide information in a consistent format.

Proposal Content

The investment proposal document should contain the following:

- Cover sheet with spaces for signatories to indicate approval
- Introduction
- Summary of investment and returns
- Relation to strategic plan; impact on future product demand, competitive strategy, and manufacturing goals
- Market evaluation and volumes
- Product response and specification, characteristics, targets (plus customer cost of ownership)
- Alternative courses of action, including risk-management plan
- Investment appraisal over investment period and life cycle
- Sensitivity analysis and risks and opportunities

Appendixes should provide:

- Volumes and market-share projections, incremental and substitutional effects
- Investment details (asset categories, phasing)
- R&D and engineering time and cost summary
- Manufacturing throughput times
- Unit prices and costs (including customer cost of ownership and quality-cost assessment)
- Unit prices and costs comparison versus products replaced
- Unit prices and costs comparison versus competition
- Product profit and loss statement and balance sheet
- Evaluation of cash flow and discounted cash flow
- Timing charts, milestones
- Key factors weighting chart

Sources of Information for Proposal

All business functions supply information used to prepare the investment proposal.

Sales and Marketing contributes volumes and market-share projections; product characteristics and specification; prices and discounts; life span; substitution and complementary effects; competitor assessment; spares and service criteria (with Quality Assurance); literature and manuals; and launch requirements.

Manufacturing contributes capacity and sourcing assumptions; facility and worker needs; labor efficiencies, scrap assumptions; preproduction and launch volumes and costs; and stock levels (with Sales and Marketing).

Engineering provides specifications and drawings; estimates of time, cost, and investment; timing plans; and tooling requirements (with Manufacturing).

Purchasing provides the cost of new materials and components.

Quality Assurance contributes warranty and service costs.

Finance contributes information on unit costs; cost of capital; working-capital requirements; fixed-assets utilization; overheads and bases of apportionment; exchange-rate forecasts; grants and taxation; and depreciation and amortization policy.

Project Manager supplies information on key milestones and achievement targets, and value-for-money criteria.

ABANDONMENT ANALYSIS

This section summarizes abandonment theory and discusses some of the operational problems of applying it.

What Is Abandonment Analysis?

Abandonment analysis is an extension of normal DCF investment appraisal techniques that allows the management accountant to assess whether it is more profitable to continue or to abandon a project.

At some time, a project must be abandoned either because the physical limits of the equipment have been reached or because current and future cash flows no longer justify it. In his article "Capital Investment under Uncertainty with Abandonment Options," Charles Bonini states that "it is not necessary for cash flows to become negative before the project is abandoned."[1]

Abandonment itself may produce positive cash flows, such as tax benefits of depreciation write-offs, sale of fixed assets, and reduction of working capital on the use of space by more profitable projects. In such cases, the project would be abandoned if estimated future cash flows (appropriately discounted) did not exceed the current abandonment value. The results of abandonment analysis within a product life-cycle review model significantly affect the quality of information available for inclusion in cash-flow projections.

---

1. Bonini, "Capital Investment under Uncertainty," 39.

When to Apply Abandonment Analysis

At every step of the product life-cycle review after the investment proposal, management should consider the advisability of continuing or abandoning an investment project. Abandonment analysis should be a tool used throughout a product's life cycle after the investment proposal.

Problems of Applying Abandonment Analysis

Volume and Accuracy of Projected Revenue Streams. The difficulties associated with projecting future revenues and costs for use in abandonment analysis are equal to those encountered in all investment appraisal techniques. The extension of new-product appraisal by abandonment analysis will increase the demands on financial and nonfinancial management to provide accurate and substantive information.

Identification and Quantification of Abandonment Costs. Information regarding the future resale price of capital equipment is not easily obtained and the data will be imprecise because it is a forecast.

Vested Interests and Negative Attitudes. There is a danger in abandonment analysis that the quality of information and the level of interest shown in the findings of such analysis will be affected by the involvement of project sponsors and those heavily committed to a particular investment. The potential distortion of abandonment analysis because of nonfinancial considerations cannot be ignored.

Cumbersome and Inappropriate Mechanics. The optimal abandonment decision rule is to determine the cash flows of current operations and to compare those with the cash flows for abandonment. The alternative with the highest expected net present value should be chosen. This rule is difficult to implement, because of the numerous possible cash flow scenarios. This technique should not be the only input to the decision. The rule is of value because it forces a firm to evaluate important criteria.

Intangibles. Some products are included in a product line even if they are unprofitable. Reasons for this include the impact on other product sales, the public's perception of the business in terms of product offering, and the retention of expertise.

Despite these disadvantages, the benefits to be obtained from a more realistic approach to project abandonment can only improve the product-planning process. The inclusion of abandonment analysis in the product life-cycle review will identify at an early stage projects that may be expected to fail in terms of achieving the required return on investment.

WHOLE-LIFE COST CONSIDERATIONS

This section presents a whole-life view of the factors of technology accounting throughout the product life cycle.

Whole-life costs can be defined as the costs to the customer "from the cradle to the grave." In many industries, acquisition costs in the form of research, development, and production form only a small part of the whole-life costs; the cost incurred by the consumer in operating the product is often greater than the acquisition costs. Customers are becoming increasingly demanding in terms of reliability and maintainability of products. This places increased emphasis on whole-life costing.

At present, even the best cost accounting system addresses only acquisition costs. However, a significant part of ownership costs are decided early in design. It is, therefore, at this stage that good project control and adequate feedback from production and in-service phases will eventually lead to highly competitive products launched in the market. Figure 5.6 emphasizes the importance of linking early development with the cost of ownership.

There are many major cost drivers in the cost of ownership. Some only become apparent after diligent research and months of experience with new projects or techniques. Others include unit production costs, failure rates, repair costs, spares costs, and buffer stock levels to maintain certain systems availability.

All these aspects are within the control of the company and should be considered part of the CMS design. Parametric models are commercially available to translate these factors into whole-life

Figure 5.6
Whole-Life Costs

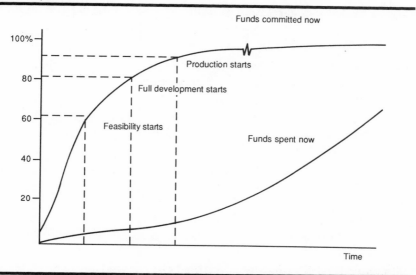

cost estimates. Figure 5.6 illustrates how such models are used at the design stage of the product life-cycle model.

REFERENCES AND FURTHER READINGS

Adar, A., A. Barnea, and B. Lev. "A Comprehensive Cost-Volume-Profit Analysis under Uncertainty." *The Accounting Review* (January 1977): 137–149.

Armitage, H. *Linking Management Information Systems with Computer Technology.* Hamilton, Ontario: Society of Management Accountants of Canada, September 1985.

Bonini, C. P. "Capital Investment under Uncertainty with Abandonment Options." *Journal of Financial & Quantitative Analysis* (March 1977): 39–54.

Demski, J. S. "Optimal Performance Measurement." *The Journal of Accounting Research* (Autumn 1972): 243–258.

Denna, E. L., and W. E. McCarthy. "An Events-Accounting Foundation for DSS Use." In *Proceedings of the NATO Advanced Study Institute* (Maratea, Italy), 1986.

Folger, H. Russell. "Ranking Techniques and Capital Budgeting." *The Accounting Review* (January 1972): 134–143.

Hayes, R. H., and S. C. Wheelwright. "Linking Manufacturing Process and Product Life Cycles." *Harvard Business Review* (January–February 1979): 133–140.

Jacobs, F. "When and How to Use Statistical/Cost Variance Investigation Techniques." *Cost and Management* (January/February 1983): 26–32.

Kaplan, R. S. "Measuring Manufacturing Performance: A New Challenge for Managerial Accounting Research." *The Accounting Review* (October 1983): 686–704.

McCarthy, William E. "The REA Accounting Model: A Generalized Framework for Accounting Systems in a Shared Data Environment." *The Accounting Review* (July 1982): 554–578.

Richardson, P. R., and J. R. M. Gordon. "Measuring Total Manufacturing Performance." *Sloan Management Review* (Winter 1980): 47–58.

Sundem, G. L. "Evaluating Simplified Capital Budgeting Models Using a Time-State Preference Metric." *The Accounting Review* (April 1974): 306–320.

CHAPTER 6

CMS Performance Measurement *

A s mentioned in Chapter 3, the ultimate goal of a manufacturing company is to be recognized by customers and the industry as a dependable supplier of products that excel in terms of quality, cost, functionality, and timely availability in world markets.

Reaching this goal is a matter of planning and executing corporate business strategies based on analyses of company and competitor strengths and weaknesses. The approach that a given company takes may be based on such factors as desired profitability, return-on-investment, cash flow, increasing market share, or reducing total costs. Steps along the way might be, for instance, reducing overhead costs, improving performance quality, or meeting delivery requirements.

Once an improvement strategy is established, a company must translate the critical success factors into manufacturing facility operational requirements. Implementing these requirements continually compels manufacturers to improve the efficiency and effectiveness of all resources, including the optimal use of "new era" manufacturing processes and techniques like JIT, FMS, islands of automation, and CIM. A key factor in ensuring the successful implementation of a company's strategic plan is performance measurement, which measures business and plant performance in relation to the goals and objectives developed in the planning process; provides timely information for identifying and eliminating activities that add no value; and provides timely information on causal factors that may lead to manufacturing improvements. Performance measurement, then, plays an important role in improving the efficiency of the facility.

---

*Most of this chapter was developed and written by Lawrence J. Utzig of General Electric Company.

Value is added to a product only when it is being processed (process time). Activities associated with move time and wait time add unnecessary cost to products and should be eliminated. Material that makes long moves from process to process or that must wait for setup, inspection, buffering, or process disruptions is visible evidence that there is opportunity for improvement in the system. Most such non-value-added activity is inherent in the typical job or batch-processing shop because of functional layouts, long setups, unsynchronized flow, material shortages, quality checks, centralized stockrooms, scheduling-system problems, measurement-system inefficiencies, and so on. These latent inefficiencies interrupt the production process and result in long lead times.

As job shops take steps to operate more like continuous-flow shops by running smaller lots through cells and point-of-use processes, there is an opportunity to establish simpler and more compatible measurements. This enhances both day-to-day and long-range elimination of non-value-added costs and performance tracking.

Many performance measurements in traditional manufacturing are not compatible with continuous-flow manufacturing. They do not encourage elimination of non-value-added costs to facilitate the transition to continuous-flow manufacturing. For instance, labor standards include an allowance for "unavoidable delays," and setup costs are often treated as value-added direct labor and included as efficiency measurements. Measuring the efficiency of individual operators and foremen encourages unnecessary production of WIP inventory, while machine-utilization measurements encourage keeping machines running beyond demands of the daily schedule. Some inventory-valuation procedures encourage high inventories to overliquidate overhead and increase income. Purchase-price variance measurements sometimes emphasize material-vendor pricing rather than quality. Thus, some measurements encourage suboptimization, which adversely affects total plant performance.

Perfection in continuous-flow manufacturing means configuring a production process so that the time required to flow parts from suppliers through the shop to shipping is only as long as the value-added time in the manufacturing process. It means continually measuring and attacking interruptions in the system (non-value-added time). If lead time were equal to value-added time, exact needs would be met at the exact time at all stages in the production process. There would be zero time between operations, and all processes would be perfect and perfectly balanced. The lot size would be 1, and WIP inventory would be the sum of all parts being processed at any given time (approaching zero inventory). This is the objective of continuous-flow manufacturing, and this is why all waste related to material waiting and moving must be eliminated.

MEASUREMENT PRINCIPLES

Strategic planning must include a structured approach to performance monitoring and measurement. Just as key business objectives are identified, evaluated, and ranked according to importance in the strategic plan, so must performance measures be assessed. The CAM-I CMS Conceptual Design incorporates a flexible, goal-oriented methodology for establishing a performance measurement strategy.

Performance measures should support company goals and be adaptable to business needs. They should yield cost-effective and timely data on all significant activities of the company, be easy to apply, and be accepted at all personnel levels.

Consistency with Company Goals

Performance measures should be consistent with company goals and objectives and should consider both internal and external factors required to achieve these objectives. Performance measures must, at all levels of manufacturing and management, provide a link between business activities and the business plan. The strategic plan, therefore, must be stated in terms that apply throughout the various levels of manufacturing and reporting responsibilities. The four levels in the management hierarchy include market, business, plant, and shop floor. The performance measurement hierarchy is pictured in Figure 6.1.

Market Level. A company should measure its competitive position with regard to the performance of the economy as a whole and the

Figure 6.1
Performance Measurement Hierarchy

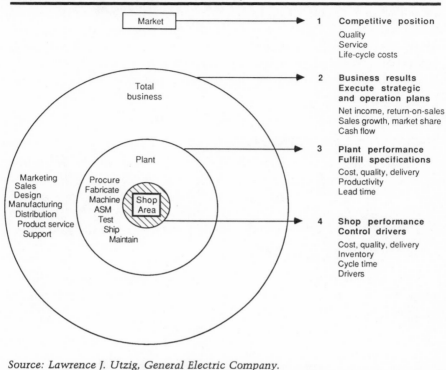

Source: Lawrence J. Utzig, General Electric Company.

industry in which a company operates. These measures might include quality, service, life-cycle cost, and market share.

Business Level. A company should measure its business results, which will be reflected in its current profit level and its future profit potential (as embodied in technologically superior assets). The business goals should be stated in terms of the critical success factors, which should be established for each department. These measures might include net income, return-on-sales, market share, and cash flow.

Plant Level. A company should translate the critical success factors into shop measures, expressed in both financial and nonfinancial terms. These measures might include cost, quality, delivery, productivity, and lead time.

Shop-floor Level. A company should measure the shop performance. The marketing, engineering, and plant-support activities that affect shop performance will be primarily nonfinancial.

Adaptability to Business Needs

Performance measures should be adaptable to changing business needs as well as to a variety of objectives. Companies must often satisfy different (often conflicting) objectives simultaneously. Performance measures must, therefore, be prioritized according to those strategic success factors deemed most critical. Attention should focus on *these measures* as they relate directly to the stated goals, avoiding undue emphasis on other measures.

As business needs change, performance measures should change. Measures must be reviewed and reranked, as necessary, to reflect the currently relevant critical success factors. As new measures are added, existing measures should be reviewed, modified, discounted, or discontinued (if no longer relevant). Performance measures should change *only* as a result of changing business needs, not as a result of changes in management style.

Measurement of Significant Activities

Performance measures should be established at the activity level. They must reflect those activities that are significant to the company. Each company must define significant activities based on its business objectives and operating environment.

These activities should be classified as value-added or non-value-added. At the manufacturing level, value-added activities are process activities and non-value-added activities are those associated with inspection, waiting, and movement (see Table 6.1). The first step in eliminating non-value-added activities is to understand the drivers that cause these activities (see Table 6.2). The next step is to establish the performance measures. These might include lead time, inventory, conversion cost, quality, schedule performance, and machine hours per part (see Figure 6.2).

Table 6.1
Lead-Time Analysis to Reduce Waste Drivers

PROCESS	INSPECTION	MOVE	WAIT
Process technology	QA plan	Plant layout	Quality problems/repairing
Equipment capability	Part quality	Parts routing	Equipment problems
Product design	Inspection method	Rerouting	Tooling problems
Methods instruction	Documentation requirements	Rescheduling	Design problems
	Inspection skill	Stock points	Setup/Lot size (in queue)
	Product design	Repair	Scheduling/routing/accumulating
		Changes	Absenteeism
		Door locations	Parts shortages
		Aisles	Unbalance
			Build ahead/early
			Equipment capacity
			Changes
			Container size

Source: Lawrence J. Utzig, General Electric Company.

Ease of Application

Performance measures should be easy to apply. Once the significant activities have been identified, the measures established for those activities should be easy to understand, few in number, and quantifiable. Many measurements are best expressed in terms of quantities like time or number of transactions, but these quantities should be expressible in financial terms, as well, if required.

Top-Down Acceptability

Performance measures should help establish congruence between organizational and company objectives. A company must recognize the role of performance measures in modifying the behavior of functional managers. The axiom "You get what you measure" ap-

Table 6.2
Drivers of Non-Value-Added Activities

PROCESS	INSPECTION	MOVE	WAIT
Machine	Inspectors	Material handling	Troubleshooting/repairing/checking
Fabricate	Inspection equipment	Handling equipment	Sorting
Assemble	Inspection plans	Damaged parts	Reload/unload
Setup	Defect recording		Expediting
Check	Defect reporting		Storing/attending/accumulating
Load	Defect analysis		Unplanned operator time
Unload	Defect correction		Recording/reporting/distributing
			Extra clerical
			Redesign/retest
			Inventory carrying cost
			Damaged parts
			Space productivity
			Managing wasteful activities
			Re-do changed work
			Obsolete parts
			Lost parts

Source: Lawrence J. Utzig, General Electric Company.

plies. The lowest-level organization should support the attainment of specific goals and objectives established by top management in the strategic-planning process. A top-down approach should be utilized to define performance measures that reinforce optimal behavior at all levels of the company.

Each performance measure should be totally within the accountability of the person or group performing the activity to be measured. The measures should span the responsibility of the activity without overlapping the responsibilities of other activities.

Measures should be specifically defined and expressed in relevant units. The method of quantification and the purpose of key per-

Figure 6.2
Performance Measurements

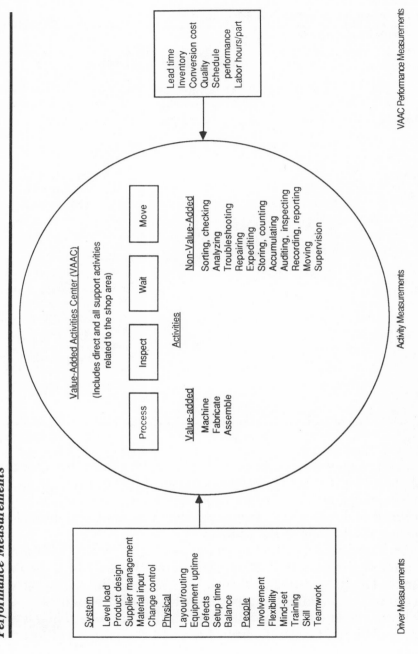

Source: Lawrence J. Utzig, General Electric Company.

formance measures should be communicated to the appropriate tiers within the company. The relations between functional organization goals and company goals should be explained. This may require an ongoing investment in training and active group participation to ensure understanding and consistent application.

Results of all performance measures should be visible to as many people as possible to focus attention, to encourage understanding, and to improve performance.

Cost Effectiveness and Timeliness

Performance data should be cost-effective, available, and timely. They should be reported on a timely basis and in a format that aids decision making. The timing of data capture and reporting must be evaluated in view of subsequent actions required, costs and benefits associated with providing the data, and validity of the data. This refers to both historical events and the future impact of those events.

For any activity, there can exist complex relationships among the people who perform the activity, the systems and procedures used, and the physical factors associated with the technology used. Although the frequent product and process advances that have occurred have been visible, the impact on performance measurement often has not been understood or modified to keep pace with these changes.

Cost is only one aspect of performance. Under the CMS Conceptual Design, greater emphasis is given to providing nonfinancial information for management reporting and decision support. The manufacturing environment is a key factor that influences the performance measurement system. As a company makes the transition from traditional manufacturing to process simplification and increased levels of automation, different aspects of performance may need to be emphasized during the transition phase as well as when the implementation has been completed.

The manufactured products are an important consideration in performance measurement. The critical tasks of manufacturing change as products move through their life cycles. Thus, different performance measures are appropriate at different times during the product life cycle.

CONTINUOUS-FLOW MEASUREMENT PLANNING

Measurement planning should begin at the very outset of a continuous-flow program. Since the plan must mesh with the overall strategy and implementation timetable, existing measurements and systems must be reviewed for compatibility with the goals to implement continuous-flow manufacturing and lead-time/waste reduction. To the degree that these systems are already designed for a repetitive manufacturing environment where production is planned and controlled on a *flow-rate* rather than a *job-order* basis, the migration to continuous flow will be simplified.

Performance measurement should support the requirements of a high-turns inventory environment. This implies that a relatively level and stable production plan has been developed, so that material can flow at an established rate. The emphasis is on meeting the plan (daily schedule), which presumes that the pipeline always contains the required *minimum* amount of materials or that they can be provided quickly; labor and machine capacity have been positioned properly; incoming and in-process quality are of a high order; and machines and tools are well maintained.

In general, computerized information systems play a lesser role in providing measurement data on the shop floor and a greater role in front-end planning functions like master scheduling, final assembly scheduling, material-requirements planning, capacity-requirements planning, and target cost.

Because the planning and control of production in a repetitive manufacturing environment is simpler than in a job-order environment, the measurements required also will be simpler. However, during the transition, which can last several years, measurements may be needed for both the traditional and continuous-flow manufacturing environments.

IMPACT ON ACCOUNTING SYSTEMS

In general, as business moves from a job-order to a flow-rate environment, and as manufacturing cells gradually replace conventional process-oriented layouts, cost control, inventory control, labor measurement, and manufacturing overhead allocation all will be simplified. Those systems that accumulate costs by discrete batch or work order will be modified as work orders give way to continuous-flow, repetitive production. The trend will be toward process costing, where the total plant, manufacturing cells, or assembly lines become the natural cost centers against which all conversion costs are accumulated. Process costs then will be allocated to products depending upon cell-labor levels, the mix produced while the cell is running, and the length of time each product spends in the cell.

With continuous-flow manufacturing, the distinction between direct and indirect labor tends to blur. Not only is indirect labor significantly reduced but direct labor is expected to perform many activities, such as material handling, inspection, and machine maintenance, that normally are considered indirect. Thus, labor standards and overhead rates will change, as will the means by which cost center overhead is applied to products. Conventionally, this is done as a percentage of actual or standard direct labor. Some businesses using JIT feel that the *total* labor required to operate and support a manufacturing cell should be measured or that machine hours provide a better basis for allocating overhead.

Conventional labor measurement will also change. Where cells couple operators on miniature "production lines," individual-efficiency measurement will yield to group-efficiency measurement. The whole concept of labor efficiency will have to be re-examined, since JIT requires operators to produce only what is scheduled. When the schedule is met, operators are expected to perform other tasks, such as maintenance and work-station cleanup. Machine efficiency, too, has an entirely different meaning under JIT. Machine idle time is expected and planned for, since continuous-flow shops are designed to be labor-limited (not machine-limited).

Inventory accounting and measurements are affected because the traditional emphasis on the value and location of WIP diminishes as JIT reduces in-process quantities and cycle times. Stage-of-completion valuation becomes relatively unimportant when cycles are measured in hours or days rather than in weeks or months.

TRADITIONAL MEASURES THAT INHIBIT PERFORMANCE

As companies move toward optimized manufacturing, the emphasis placed on current performance measures may need to shift. This

Table 6.3
Traditional Accounting Measures That Inhibit Optimized Manufacturing

MEASURE-MENT	ACTION	RESULT
Purchase price	Purchasing increases order quantity to get lower price, ignoring quality and delivery	Excess inventory; increased carrying costs; supplier with best quality and delivery may be overlooked
Machine utilization	Supervisor runs the machine in excess of daily unit requirement to maximize machine utilization	Excess inventory; wrong inventory
Setup in standards	Encourages high run quantity	Excess inventory
Scrap factor built into standard cost	Supervisor takes no action if no variance	Inflated standard; minimum scrap threshold built in
Standard cost overhead absorption	Supervisor overproduces WIP to get overhead absorption in excess of expenses	Excess inventory
Indirect/direct headcount ratio	Management, not total cost, controls the ratio	Indirect labor standards wrongly established; total cost not in control
Scrap dollars	Scrap dollars drive corrective action priority	Direct-level impact on flow hidden in dollars
Cost center reporting	Management focus is on cost centers, not activities	Opportunities to reduce costs are missed when common activities are overlooked
Labor reporting	Management focus is on direct labor, which is fixed and relatively small, instead of on overhead, which is variable and large	Missed cost-reduction opportunities; major overhead activities not exposed
Earned labor dollars	Supervisor maximizes earned labor, keeps workers busy	Excess inventory, schedule attainment gets lower priority; emphasizes output
Overhead rate	Management, not total cost, controls rate	Overhead levels improperly established; high-cost activities hidden

Source: Tom Pryor, Motorola, Inc.

170

includes such obvious moves as machine utilization to machine usage; non-value-added receive more emphasis than value-added; capacity shifting to comparison of capacity against plan; resource consumption to resource utilization.

Table 6.3 lists measures that traditionally have been used by companies as gauges of performance. Sometimes using a measure or focusing inappropriate amounts of attention on it has actually increased waste. But these measures can be valid and useful indicators if applied properly. Companies should review the measures to determine the context in which they are being applied and whether it is advisable to modify or eliminate them.

KEY PERFORMANCE MEASURES

The following performance measures generally are viewed as key measures for an advanced manufacturer:

- Lead time
- Total value-added versus non-value-added time and cost
- Schedule performance (meet daily schedule)
- Product quality
- Throughput
- Engineering change notices (ECNs)
- Machine hours per part
- Plant/equipment/tooling reliability
- Cycle time
- Broad management/worker involvement
- Problem support
- High value-added design (design to cost)
- Forecast accuracy

IMPLEMENTATION OF A PERFORMANCE MEASUREMENT SYSTEM

There are several steps a company can take to implement a performance measurement system:

- Develop a hierarchical measurement system that links business, plant, and shop-floor performance
- Identify and quantify the company's cost/performance drivers

Figure 6.3
Performance Measurement Hierarchical Conceptual Approach

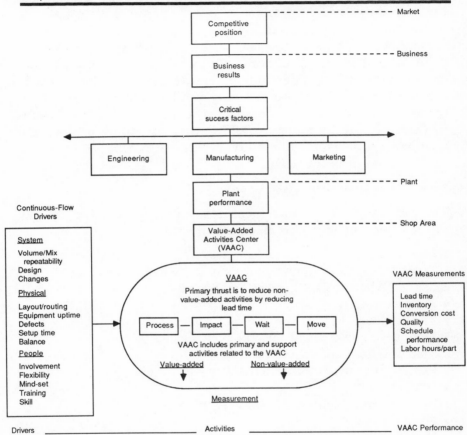

Source: *Lawrence J. Utzig, General Electric Company.*

- Identify non-value-added activities
- Eliminate inhibiting measures
- Simplify the manufacturing process to minimize or eliminate non-value-added activities

A performance measurement hierarchical conceptual approach is outlined in Figure 6.3.

FURTHER READINGS

Brown, V. H. "Rate of Return: Some Comments on Its Applicability in Capital Budgeting." *The Accounting Review* (January 1961): 50–62.

Cohen, M. A., and R. Halperin. "Optimal Inventory Order Policy for a Firm Using the LIFO Inventory Costing Method." *The Journal of Accounting Research* (Autumn 1980): 375–389.

Demski, J. S. "The Decision Implementation Interface: Effects of Alternative Performance Models." *The Accounting Review* (January 1970): 76–87.

———. "Uncertainty and Evaluation Based on Controllable Performance." *The Journal of Accounting Research* (Autumn 1976): 230–245.

Friedman, L. A., and B. R. Neuman. "The Effects of Opportunity Costs on Project Investment Decisions: A Replication and Extension." *The Journal of Accounting Research* (Autumn 1980): 407–419.

Hayes, D. C. "The Contingency Theory of Managerial Accounting." *The Accounting Review* (January 1977): 22–39.

Hughes, J. "Optimal Timing of Cost Information." *The Journal of Accounting Research* (Autumn 1979): 344–349.

Ijiri, Y., R. K. Jaedicke, and J. L. Livingstone. "The Effect of Inventory Costing Methods on Full and Direct Costing." *The Journal of Accounting Research* (Spring 1965): 63–74.

Itami, H. "Evaluation Measures and Goal Congruence under Uncertainty." *The Journal of Accounting Research* (Spring 1975): 73–96.

Jensen, R. E., and C. T. Thomas. "Statistical Analysis in Cost Measurement and Control." *The Accounting Review* (January 1968): 83–93.

Keane, S. M. "The Internal Rate of Return and the Reinvestment Fallacy." *Abacus* (January 1979): 48–55.

Langholm, O. "Cost Structure and Costing Method: An Empirical Study." *The Journal of Accounting Research* (Autumn 1965): 218–227.

Lim, W. T. "Multiple Objectives Budgeting Model: A Simulation." *The Accounting Review* (January 1978): 61–76.

Maher, M. W., and K. V. Ramanahan. "Preference Congruence, Information Accuracy, and Employee Performance: A Field Study." *The Journal of Accounting Research* (Autumn 1979): 476–503.

Moriarity, S. "Another Approach to Allocation of Joint Costs." *The Accounting Review* (October 1975): 791–795.

Ross, S. A. "The Economic Theory of Agency: The Principal's Problem." *American Economic Review* (May 1973): 134–139.

Searfoss, D. G. "Some Behavioral Aspects of Budgeting for Control: An Empirical Study." *Accounting, Organizations, and Society* (November 1976): 375–385.

Weinwurm, E. H. "The Importance of Idle Capacity Costs." *The Accounting Review* (July 1961): 418–421.

CHAPTER 7

Investment Management

T his chapter provides a conceptual design for managing investments in advanced manufacturing technologies. It begins with an overview of the principles that guided the CMS Investment Management Model design and continues with more detailed explanations of the approach, the tools, and the measurement and tracking features of the model. It also includes a preliminary version of an expert system for investment justification.

The objective of investment management is to optimize utilization of a company's resources (people, systems, technology, equipment, facilities, and finances) by identifying and implementing activities that can improve performance.

Conceptually, the CMS Investment Management Model consists of design-guiding principles, an approach to proper investment management decisions, tools for evaluating investment opportunities, and a cost-benefit tracking system to monitor and measure results of investment management decisions.

GUIDING PRINCIPLES

Several principles guided the design of the CMS Investment Management Model. They allow managers to assess activities and alternative approaches to improve a firm's future performance.

Relate Investment Decisions to Strategic Plans and Operational Goals

Sound investment management decisions must be tied to long-term strategic plans and short-term operational goals. The starting point for investment management should be the strategic plan. Investments in advanced manufacturing technology should be driven by specific requirements of the product forecast and by the company's strategy for dealing with technological change. Technology alternatives should help the company achieve the levels of performance identified in its strategic plan for the highest-priority success factors.

Invest in Integrated Technology

Investments should be considered as interrelated elements of an integrated strategy rather than as individual projects. The benefits of many advanced manufacturing technologies accrue when several of the manufacturing activities are integrated. Because these activities are synergistic, the benefits that accrue when they are linked may far outweigh the simple sum of the individual benefits of the separate activities (if not linked).

Evaluate Investment Alternatives Consistently

A consistent methodology should be used to evaluate investment alternatives. To ensure that strategic goals are satisfied, a consistent evaluation methodology should be applied to investment management decisions. This methodology should translate strategic objectives into performance targets. Technology projects should be considered in a portfolio to facilitate reaching these targets given the resource constraints.

Evaluate Investments by Financial and Nonfinancial Criteria

Investments should be evaluated according to qualitative and quantitative nonfinancial criteria as well as the traditional financial criteria. Cost and typical financial ratios such as ROI represent only one aspect of an investment. Resulting improvements in quality, throughput, and flexibility can be of vital strategic importance. Thus, such criteria should be addressed in the strategic plan and should be considered when evaluating candidate projects.

Assess Risks

The investment management process should assess the risks associated with both the total investment strategy and individual projects. Each investment should be assessed for economic, technological, and implementation risks. Economic risk represents the risk of not achieving projected economic benefits. Technological risk depends primarily on whether the technology is commercially available or must be developed. It is influenced by the estimated life of the new technology and its compatibility with a facility's existing technology. Human factors form the basis of implementation risks.

Utilize Cost and Performance Data Provided by CMS

CMS must provide the cost and performance data required for ongoing monitoring of the investment. The cost management system must be able to monitor and report the data necessary to measure the success of investment strategies. This applies both at the level of individual investment projects and at the corporate strategy level.

THE CMS INVESTMENT MANAGEMENT METHODOLOGY

Managers should evaluate investment options by applying a consistent methodology that identifies those projects most complementary to the company's strategic plan. This section describes guidelines for adopting and implementing such a methodology.

Extract Required Information from Strategic Plan

The strategic plan should provide investment managers with these primary inputs: business objectives, product forecasts, and a competitive strategy.

Business Objectives. Investment managers should look to the strategic plan for business objectives regarding such measures as market share, revenue growth, and profitability. These objectives should be clearly stated and expressed in quantifiable terms (e.g., "a 5 percent increase in market share"). The strategic plan objectives will later be translated into specific targets required to achieve the objectives. The specific targets address such critical success factors as cost, quality, flexibility, throughput, delivery, and responsiveness to sudden demand changes (e.g., a 10 percent reduction in costs, or a three-day reduction in delivery period).

Product Forecasts. Investment managers need forecasts, because advances in product technology set a company's products apart from those of the competition. New features or improved materials provide opportunities to capture market share. But this is a two-edged sword: a company may not be able to produce such features or use such materials with its existing manufacturing facilities.

The strategic planning process should provide a forecast of demand for, and performance of, those products. The plan should provide for translating these forecasts into the required manufacturing capabilities at the time they are needed. For example, in the aerospace industry, forecasts of higher fuel costs and improved aircraft performance underscore the need for lighter, stronger materials such as fiber composites. An airplane manufacturer's strategic plan must therefore incorporate the investment strategies and schedules necessary to manufacture, use, and support these new materials.

Competitive Strategies. A company can adopt any of three types of competitive strategies to fight market obsolescence: proactive, technology-responsive, and reactive.

With a *proactive strategy*, a company can become a technology leader and set the industry standard, with the resultant reward of potentially large profit margins and market share until competitors upgrade their facilities. The risk of this strategy is that a company may invest many resources in what turns out to be a technological failure or a successful technology that either is not economical or fails to give the forecast strategic advantage.

With a *technology-responsive strategy*, a company can monitor advances and invest in technologies *after* the value of a technology has been shown. The advantage of this approach is that it allows a company to focus resources on less risky technologies, with minimal time delay in implementing the new technologies in the factory. The risk of this approach is the potential loss of market share to technology leaders. Such a risk is particularly high for revolutionary technologies that require significant plant modernization.

With a *reactive strategy* a company can wait until a technology is fully developed and becomes available "off the shelf." The advantage of this strategy is that there is very little technological risk. The risk of this strategy is significant loss of market share and potentially lower profit margins.

Because of the variety of products and processes of most businesses today, company planners must choose a mix of the three competitive strategies. For example, the proactive strategy is necessary in those cases where revolutionary technologies dictate competition in a particular market. In the aerospace industry, for example, building composite airplanes renders some metal-cutting and joining operations obsolete while at the same time requiring not only newer cutting and joining technologies but also significant improvements in tolerances and process control from engineering to production.

Companies also must be technology-responsive to techniques that may have a limited, short-term, negative effect on customer satisfaction but a significant influence on technological obsolescence in the intermediate term. In such cases, they have the luxury of monitoring technological advances and of waiting to adopt a technology until after it has been shown to work. Meanwhile, they can compete on other bases, such as service, delivery, or reliability, to reduce loss of market share until the newer technology is in place.

Finally, some technologies can increase manufacturing productivity without radically altering competition. Companies assume very few technical risks for such projects but stand to gain less as well, since long-term benefits are limited.

Identify Non-Value-Added Costs and Cost Drivers

The objectives of optimized manufacturing can be achieved only by identifying non-value-added costs and cost drivers and then applying advanced manufacturing technologies to eliminate them. Non-value-added costs are parasitic: they add cost to a product without increasing its value. Cost drivers are the primary determinants of costs within a business activity or manufacturing process. CMS must continually provide timely data on these costs and the forces driving them.

Manufacturers strive to structure their activities to apply resources efficiently to make competitive products with regard to cost, quality, functionality, and market timing. Technologies that significantly improve these product characteristics are excellent candidates for investment. When management must choose among production technologies that are apparently equally qualified, one way to evaluate the best alternative is to analyze the effects of the different methods on total life-cycle costs.

The CMS Functional Model described in Chapter 3 provides a consistent, structured hierarchical definition of functions, activities, and tasks. It also identifies opportunities for cost management and cost control at each activity level. To understand the impact of activities on the cost and performance of other activities, a successful investment management strategy must hierarchically define the business functions as presented in the CMS Functional Model. These activities should be defined using a standardized list of generic activities to facilitate the linking of the source activity with the benefactors' activity and its impact on the total general ledger (accounting) cost.

The number of activities should be generic to reduce the number of general ledger accounts. The number of accounts needed to define a company's organization (function, activity, and task) optimally should be defined at the level where the cost of the additional dispersion of the data exceeds the benefits of its accuracy. A life-cycle focus requires the establishment of a strategic five- to ten-year budget for each significant cost element at the functional or activity level and a one- to two-year budget at the microactivity or task level over the product life cycle of each product line. As Figure 7.1 shows, the activities from engineering conception through the manufacturing and product logistics support are time-phased and interrelated. All fifteen business activities defined in the CMS Engineering/Manufacturing Activities Model for each product line not only can have different cost profiles but also can be at different phases of the product life cycle.

To manage a multiproduct, multifunctional business enterprise optimally, information is needed on what the time-phased cost profile should be for each business activity and where on the life cycle it should be (is) at all times for each end-item product (line). This function is known as life-cycle management. There is a growing consensus that proper front-end investment in strategic planning means concurrently designing the product and process, starting at the system level and hierarchically driving these requirements down to the piece-part operation level. It is critical to design not only for producibility and automation but also for automated product/process verification (closed-loop, real-time feedback process control) and for maintainability, reliability, and supportability in the field. Figure 7.2 shows the impact of improving the engineer-

Figure 7.1
Total Life-Cycle Cost Profile

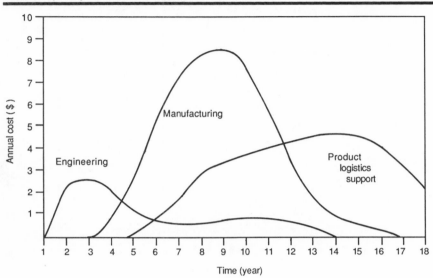

Source: Richard L. Engwall, Westinghouse Electric Corporation.

ing function (viewed as an investment) on the total life-cycle cost profile. Traditionally, companies sacrifice significant long-term profits for insignificant immediate profits. The product line should be managed so that prior business-decision benefits pay for the additional front-end investment needed to fund new emerging products. Generally speaking, the considerable leverage expected from making the proper front-end investment can be seen in the generalized cost profile net change projected in Figure 7.2. Cost management systems must therefore be capable of planning, budgeting, accumulating, reporting, and controlling costs to the level of detail necessary to optimize management's investment decisions so as to maximize both short-term profit and long-term growth and profitability objectives.

Establish Performance Targets

Once non-value-added costs and cost drivers are identified, management must establish improvement objectives for the perfor-

Figure 7.2
Impact of Front-End Investment on Total Life-Cycle Cost

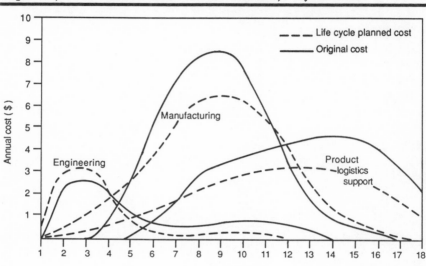

Source: Richard L. Engwall, Westinghouse Electric Corporation.

mance measures, such as product cost, quality, flexibility, and throughput. When aiming at these targets, management must understand the sensitivity of the company's markets. One market may be very cost-conscious, while another may be motivated by quality. For example, if the objective is a "5 percent increase in market share," the best way to achieve it is through such targets as 10 percent reduction in costs, 5 percent increase in quality, or a one-week decrease in production time.

Whatever the analysis, it must employ a top-down approach that drives company goals from top management to the lowest level by defining specific targets for performance improvement. The gap between goals and current performance represents an improvement opportunity. Innovations, cost-reduction opportunities, and quality improvements should continue to be encouraged from the bottom up.

One important element in establishing performance targets is to identify changes in total manufacturing cost. Advanced manufacturing technologies will affect many of an organization's factors of production, other than just direct labor and the cost of equipment. Automation significantly increases support activities such as maintenance, process engineering, facilities engineering, and data processing. On the other hand, automation can reduce inventory, floor-space requirements, and planning and control costs. For this reason, the effects of implementing advanced manufacturing technologies must be analyzed to determine the cost-behavior patterns for all the major factors of production.

The starting point for the analysis should be the strategic plan. After the hierarchically organized cost data (step 2) are matched with the strategic plan (step 1), performance targets can be established for both short- and long-term strategies. Four critical performance targets should be reviewed: (1) product cost, (2) improved quality, (3) throughput, and (4) flexibility.

Product Cost. Product cost should be measured by identifying the changes to directly traceable revenues and costs. One measure of the net effect on revenue and costs is operating margin. Operating margin is gross sales versus cost of goods sold, or operating profit divided by gross sales. It is positively influenced by controlling costs relative to sales value for a given investment.

The operating margin can be improved by reducing non-value-added cost; for example, by improving manufacturing process to realize better process yield; by reducing scrap, rework, and repair costs; and by reducing setup and run costs. The higher the quality level, the lower the maintenance and support costs are to operate the product and therefore the higher the sales price can be maintained relative to cost.

Improved Quality. There are three important considerations of quality accounting: (1) performance to specifications, (2) design for quality, and (3) defect prevention. Ensuring that products perform to specifications is primarily a function of the inspection process. Sophisticated technologies now being developed will improve the inspection process.

The design-for-quality dimension focuses on the importance of the engineering function in designing products to minimize or prevent quality problems, by designing for producibility.

A goal of defect prevention is to build the product correctly the first time—a goal that focuses on the importance of the manufacturing process in preventing defects. This is best achieved by using in-line, real-time, automated inspection, which flags potential problems *before* defective products emerge.

Throughput. Three important dimensions of the product delivery cycle are: (1) engineering design and development, (2) production, and (3) customer delivery. Engineering design and development includes the time from product specification until the release of the product design to manufacturing. Production includes the product throughput. When evaluating the impact of a technology on production throughput, it is important to consider not only the process affected but also the overall factory throughput. Too often the throughput improvements in an individual process are offset to varying degrees by bottleneck processes in other parts of the factory.

The customer delivery cycle includes the time from the manufacturer's shipping dock to the customer's site plus the customer's acceptance cycle. While the former is normally beyond the scope of advanced manufacturing technologies, the customer's acceptance cycle is directly affected.

Flexibility. Flexibility can be achieved as a middle strategy between specialized, dedicated equipment and general-purpose machines. Flexible systems are developed to facilitate product-line manufacturing rather than product-specific manufacturing. Three dimensions of flexibility are: (1) economies of scope, (2) economies of product line (economies of time), and (3) economies of capability. Economies of scope provide the potential for low-cost production for a large mix of low-volume products. These economies are possible as the result of automated setup, which facilitates an Economic Order Quantity (EOQ) of 1.

Economies of product line allow for significant flexibility within a product line to accommodate changeover product redesigns and engineering change notices. This flexibility enables a company to respond economically to the shorter life cycle demanded by the marketplace. It must be kept in mind that this flexibility is bounded by the product line. If changes make an entire product line obsolete, switching to new product lines can be expensive and require a considerable amount of time.

Economies of capability result from the reprogramming of capabilities to serve as backups to other similar machines. This product capability can augment other product lines during lead production periods.

Identify Candidate Technologies

A company should identify advanced manufacturing technologies consistent with its strategic objectives by surveying both the market and technologies already in the facility. As candidate technologies are identified, an evaluation process begins. A process-flow activity analysis defines the affected manufacturing functions' inputs, outputs, controls, and mechanisms. This establishes the baseline cost, quality, and throughput.

The CMS Manufacturing Practices Profile provides guidelines for evaluating candidate technologies in traditional, process-simplification, islands of automation, CIM, and optimized manufacturing environments. The evaluation illustrates how new technologies change the characteristics of the affected functions.

Analyze Risks of Candidate Technologies

Each candidate technology should be evaluated for economic, technological, and implementation risks. In addition, a risk-management plan for those factors that can significantly impact project outcome should be developed.

Economic Risk. In some cases, a candidate technology may not yield the projected economic benefits because of such factors as legislative trends, inflation-rate changes, interest-rate changes, competition from other companies, and time and resource constraints.

Technological Risk. It is possible that a candidate technology will fail to achieve the desired manufacturing benefits. Higher risks are associated with leading-edge applications. For critical systems, management may need to provide contingency plans. Technological risk factors include hardware failure, software failure, lack of vendor support, contingency requirements, and communication-facility failures.

Human Resource Implementation Risk. Knowledge skills and attitudes form the basis of human resources implementation risks. Human resource implementation risks include employee attitudes and skills; personnel education and training/retraining; technical support staff learning curve; employee reward system; organizational impact; integrating available data, material, personnel; and customer acceptance.

Risk-Management Plans. These procedures are developed for a candidate technology to allow management to reduce risk and maximize benefits. Such a plan is developed after identifying the significant risk factors that impact the project outcome. The identification process is a sensitivity analysis of the risk factors. To promote user acceptance and strategic sponsorship, the plan should be developed at the lowest possible decision-making level. The risk-management plan should reflect potential risks, anticipate contingencies, and track expected benefits.

Evaluate Alternative Investment Opportunities

Management should combine information from the strategic plan with knowledge of the candidate technologies to evaluate investment alternatives. Using an iterative approach, management then should select the investment portfolio that optimizes performance with the given resources.

Many factors influence the selection of investment opportunities. Traditionally, companies have focused on short-term investment benefits (profits per share) using quantitative financial information (ROI, NPV), to make yes-or-no investment decisions. Forward-looking companies, however, have also used nonfinancial quantitative measures (throughput, process yield) and qualitative criteria (product obsolescence, basic R&D) to evaluate such opportunities.

One way to assess risk and performance when evaluating investment alternatives is to use a multiple-attribute decision model. Such a model combines the attributes of the critical factors to yield a weighted score for a given investment approach. The attributes include the strategic weight, expected impact, and confidence of achieving performance goals. Managers should apply the model to each candidate technology or combination of technologies. The model would show, by virtue of the scores obtained, which project or set of projects would maximize performance.

Select an Investment Portfolio

Technologies selected for investment would be a portfolio of investment opportunities that would maximize total company performance (within resource constraints). The steps for compiling an investment portfolio are as follows:

- Determine a portfolio of projects that meet the overall strategic objectives.
- Define the total costs and benefits of the entire portfolio.
- Assess the risks of the individual projects as well as the risks of the total portfolio. (Economic risks can be reduced when synergistic projects are integrated.)
- Maximize the project benefits within resource constraints. If the requirements exceed the resources, mix the projects internally.

Portfolio Composition. Decision makers should use the portfolio approach because isolated candidate projects often are, or can be, component parts of larger computer-integrated manufacturing systems. For example, a company may not be able to justify implementing an item master-record database solely on the basis of its effect on a customer order-processing system. However, if the company's strategic plan calls for a transition to CIM systems, there may be no choice but to establish such a database or to tie in with one which is already available or under development. Factors that influence portfolio composition include project activities, technological synergies, and schedule considerations.

Impact on Other Manufacturing Functions. New technologies in an investment portfolio will affect manufacturing functions from engineering design through production. The effects on manufacturing functions must be assessed to identify the cause-and-effect relations between investment and operations. Activity inputs, outputs, controls, and mechanisms should be reviewed.

Impact on Operational Performance. Investments in technology affect operational performance. Sometimes the effects are synergistic: a CAD or a CAM system each may contribute small positive improvements to manufacturing operations if implemented separately; however, combined into a CIM system, their total effect could be greater than the sum of the individual benefits. On the other hand, some technologies that individually exhibit positive effects may actually produce *counteractive* effects when combined. For example, a manufacturing scheduling system and a flexible manufacturing system would each work to reduce WIP inventory within a work cell. However, the improvement potential of either technology would be less after implementation of the other, because the total base for improvement would be less (shared).

Analyzing such effects may require the use of structured information-flow or systems research tools (such as computer simulation) to achieve meaningful results *prior to implementing the technologies.*

Schedule Implementation. Investment projects in a portfolio should be evaluated for their "fit" to the factory automation timetable in the strategic plan. Projects may be scheduled on the basis of economics (availability of capital, customer orders, capacity) and the need for supporting technologies.

The most cost-effective scheduling for CIM implementation depends on integrating computer systems to provide real-time control of information and material through every process step. Process automation is most cost-effective with real-time control of material and information to provide the feedback necessary for automatic monitoring and process control.

Establish a Cost-Benefit Tracking System

A cornerstone of investment management is the availability of accurate and comprehensive benefit and cost data. Cost-benefit tracking is essential for generating the data necessary to understand the cost and performance of the existing manufacturing system that is to be replaced or integrated.

Cost-benefit tracking data are essential in estimating the cost and performance of the proposed manufacturing system. However, for such information to be useful in a system that is changing from one operating method to another (as when a process is automated, or when automated processes are merged into a CIM operation), the data used to support the investment analysis and the ongoing monitoring must be consistent.

The purpose of cost-benefit tracking is to monitor the critical cost and performance measures for each significant manufacturing function or process targeted for automation. The critical cost and performance elements are the same elements used for investment justification. The development, implementation, and use of a cost-benefit tracking system involve:

- Establishing the critical data elements (both cost and performance measures) to be tracked
- Assessing current availability of cost-benefit data
- Developing a cost-benefit data-validation methodology
- Designing a conceptual cost-benefit tracking system
- Validating cost models by comparing actual results with cost baselines, then analyzing any variances
- Developing procedures for responding to variances by taking corrective actions
- Designing a cost-benefit reporting system
- Installing the system
- Using the feedback to evaluate performance

A cost-benefit tracking system should ensure that cost and performance measures are compatible with internal and external requirements. Its data must be auditable and verifiable. It should track costs and benefits long enough to determine whether the projected savings have been achieved.

THE MULTIPLE-ATTRIBUTE DECISION MODEL (MADM)*

The Multiple-Attribute Decision Model is an example of a tool that helps managers make cost-effective investment decisions. It provides a weighted ranking for a project by reviewing selected critical factors against policy input from management. Critical factors to be reviewed are financial–quantitative, nonfinancial–quantitative, and qualitative.

---

* MADM is based on work done by Richard L. Engwall of Westinghouse Electric Corporation.

Rules

The MADM methodology implements the following design rules.

Minimize factors. Only a minimal number of factors should be included for comparison. High-level factors are necessary for comparing independent projects.

Factors should be rank-ordered and independent. The factor categories should be rank-ordered. All factors that can be quantified as financial should be. The categories are financial–quantitative, nonfinancial–quantitative, and qualitative.

Compare projects after evaluating them independently. Each project should be evaluated independently to arrive at a project-specific value. This value is then compared to values calculated for the other candidate projects.

Weight critical factors according to their relative importance to management. The weight of a critical factor is based on its importance to management, expressed as a percentage. The sum of all weights (the complete list of critical factors) equals 100; therefore, the weight for a given factor is a percentage of the total. This method renders the weighting understandable at a glance.

Value critical factors according to their risk in a capabilities matrix. The value for a particular critical factor is based on management priorities. Values are unique for each specific factor. For example, if the critical factor is throughput times, the matrix might look like this:

THROUGHPUT TIME	VALUE
0–2 days	1
3–5 days	2
6–9 days	3
10–15 days	4
> 15 days	5

Assign risk at 95 percent confidence level, where the critical factor's performance is at highest risk. The risk factor represents the extreme point for the expected probability at 95 percent confidence level, where performance is at highest risk. The input must be provided by people who know the process well. A high risk could be as low as 50 percent, which (if chosen) would deflate the assigned value for the critical factor. Wherever feasible, decision tables should be designed and used to apply the confidence factor objectively.

Use these factors for financial–quantitative critical values. The suggested factors for the financial–quantitative critical values are net present value (NPV), level of investment per time period, level of savings per time period, other, and operating margin. These items were selected because they represent a minimal number of different views affecting return-on-investment. The critical factors do not introduce any new statistics but do emphasize the need to consider the differing views. NPV provides the time-phased relation of savings to investment. ROI evaluation is not required, because the listed factors collectively address all critical ROI relations.

The level of investment and savings identify the magnitude of the cash-flow streams, particularly the peak requirements relative to the company's financial constraints, its requirements for change, or both. The operating margin represents the ratio of operating costs relative to product revenue. This measure can be viewed as an indication of competitiveness.

Use these factors for nonfinancial–quantitative critical values. The suggested factors for the nonfinancial–quantitative critical values are throughput time (calendar time from start to finish of any internal task); process yield (percentage of good process output to total process output); schedule attainment (percentage of net good, actual output to total scheduled output at scheduled due date); lead time (calendar time from the start to completion of a task for external processes); and other. This set of critical values also presents a maximum set of views affecting performance measurement minimal numbers. Process yield is an anticipated measure of quality. Asset-turnover performance, which reflects not only inventory levels but also effective use of the company's capital equipment, is actually better measured as net present value and operating profit margin than as a separate factor.

Use these factors for the qualitative critical values. The suggested factors for the qualitative critical values include process, product, technology, basic R&D, and other.

Application of MADM

Strategically important matters such as introducing a new product line or process and the need for basic R&D investment should be reflected in the weights assigned during strategic planning. Table 7.1 outlines the MADM conceptual model. The methodology of evaluating multiple attributes in a consistent manner is more important than the precision of the weights assigned. However, the weights assigned should be based on the company's strategic plan. The MADM is one technique that can be employed to evaluate alternative investment scenarios. It is a structured tool that pro-

Table 7.1
MADM Conceptual Model

CRITICAL FACTOR	WEIGHT (A)	VALUE (B)	RISK (C)	TOTAL (A × B × C)

I. Financial–Quantitative
  a. Net present value
  b. Return-on-investment
  c. Level of investment
  d. Level of savings
	Establish individual weights for each criterion adding to 100% total	See individual decision tables for each criterion	0–100% per criterion	

II. Nonfinancial–Quantitative
  a. Throughput time
  b. Process yield
  c. Schedule attainment
  d. Lead time				

III. Qualitative
  a. Process
  b. Basic R&D
  c. Technology obsolescence
  d. Product obsolescence				

Total	100			

Tables 7.1–7.7 are from Richard L. Engwall, Westinghouse Electric Corporation.

vides a disciplined way to relate strategic planning with tactical decision-making needs.

To use MADM, add the weighted averages of the three types of factors. Select the values from the preassigned decision tables, multiply each value by its associated confidence level (0 to 1.0), and sum the values for each factor. Among a group of investment alternatives modeled in this way, the project with the highest total is the one that best fits the strategic plan.

Using MADM

MADM is most effective when weights and decision tables for critical factors are established early in the strategic planning process. Risk is assumed to be 100 within the 95 percent confidence interval ($\pm$ 2 sigma normal distribution).

The hypothetical examples shown in Tables 7.2, 7.3, and 7.4 illustrate how each critical factor might be evaluated. A company is assumed to have $1 billion in sales, ten product lines, high-tech military products, and a $100-million investment.

Applying Confidence Factors

Wherever feasible, managers should establish decision tables for objective evaluation of alternative risks. Experts familiar with the technologies should establish each decision matrix. In the following example, notice the confidence-level factor is based on the rela-

Table 7.2
Financial–Quantitative Example

NET PRESENT VALUE ($M)		LEVEL OF INVESTMENT ($M)		LEVEL OF SAVINGS ($M)	
< −5	0	> 20	0	0	0
−5 to −2.5	1	20 to 15	1	0 to 1	1
−2.5 to 0	2	15 to 11	2	1 to 3	2
0 to 2.5	3	11 to 8	3	3 to 5	3
2.5 to 5	4	8 to 5	4	5 to 7	4
> 5	5	5	5	7 to 10	5

Table 7.3
Nonfinancial–Quantitative Example

THROUGHPUT TIME (calendar weeks)		PROCESS YIELD (%)		SCHEDULE ATTAINMENT (%)		LEAD TIME (calendar weeks)	
> 15	1	< 85	0	< 90 or > 110	0	> 30	0
10 to 15	2	85 to 90	1	90 to 110	1	25 to 30	1
5 to 10	3	90 to 95	2	95 to 105	2	20 to 25	2
2 to 5	4	95 to 98	3	97.5 to 102.5	3	15 to 10	3
< 2	5	98 to 100	4	99 to 101	4	10 to 15	4
		100	5	100	5	< 10	5

Table 7.4
Qualitative Example

Process
Required for new product   5
Improved process capability   3
Cost reduction   1

Basic R&D
Innovative major breakthrough   5
Future technology requirement   3
Required to complete new product development   1

Technology Obsolescence
Technology leap frog   5
Required for next quantitative replacement   3
Alternative technology   1

Product Obsolescence
Technology leap frog   5
Required for next quantitative replacement   3
Alternative technology   1

Table 7.5
Confidence-Level Factor Table (1.0 = Zero Risk)

HARDWARE	NO SOFTWARE DEVELOPMENT REQUIRED	SOFTWARE DEVELOPMENT IS MINIMAL	MAJOR SOFTWARE DEVELOPMENT EFFORT IS REQUIRED
Installed and working elsewhere	1.0	0.9	0.3
Working demo	0.85	0.7	0.25
Prototype working	0.65	0.5	0.2
Requires integration of existing technologies	0.5	0.4	0.15
New concept not previously attempted or new technology required	0.4	0.3	0.05

tive technological maturity of the hardware and software. The lower the number, the lower the confidence in the attribute. Remember, these factors will be multiplied by the value of the critical factors to which they apply, thereby weighting the values. (See Table 7.5.)

MADM Example

This example illustrates the use of the model to select between two investment alternatives. The first case is a relatively low-risk stand-alone conventional technology (see Table 7.6). The second case is a high-risk flexible manufacturing system (see Table 7.7). MADM analysis shows that the flexible manufacturing system is preferable to the conventional technology *despite the fact that it is a higher-risk project.* Without an unbiased model, applied fairly and equally to both alternatives, it would be difficult for management to justify investment in new manufacturing technologies, because

Table 7.6
Scenario 1. Low-Risk Stand-Alone Conventional Technology

CRITICAL FACTOR	WEIGHT (A)	VALUE (B)	RISK (C)	TOTAL (A × B × C)
I. Financial–Quantitative				
a. Net present value	20	3	1.00	60
b. Operating profit margin	25	2	1.00	50
c. Level of investment	5	4	1.00	20
d. Level of savings	5	2	1.00	10
II. Nonfinancial–Quantitative				
a. Throughput time	7	2	1.00	14
b. Process yield	15	2	1.00	30
c. Schedule attainment	3	2	1.00	6
d. Lead time	5	2	1.00	10
III. Qualitative				
a. Process	5	1	1.00	5
b. Basic R&D	2	0	1.00	0
c. Technology obsolescence	5	2	1.00	10
d. Product obsolescence	3	0	1.00	1
Total	100			215

of the typically higher risks associated with them. But as MADM shows, there is a clear and quantifiable difference (250 versus 215). This indicates that the flexible manufacturing system best matches the strategic plan *as defined by the model's decision tables.*

COST-BENEFIT TRACKING SYSTEM

After an investment is made, sound investment management calls for cost-benefit tracking. This task provides feedback to the estimating procedures for further decisions. Cost-benefit tracking should occur with the same elements that were used to justify the investment. For technologies selected for investment, CMS should track the important cost and performance elements to ensure that forecast goals are achieved. This information will be retained for validation during the detailed design/implementation and benefits tracking activities. The information developed for the cost-benefit

Table 7.7
Scenario 2. High-Risk Flexible Manufacturing System

CRITICAL FACTOR	WEIGHT (A)	VALUE (B)	RISK (C)	TOTAL (A × B × C)
I. Financial–Quantitative				
a. Net present value	20	5	.80	80
b. Operating profit margin	25	5	.70	88
c. Level of investment	5	2	.70	7
d. Level of savings	5	4	.70	14
II. Nonfinancial–Quantitative				
a. Throughput time	7	4	.90	25
b. Process yield	15	4	.90	54
c. Schedule attainment	3	4	1.00	12
d. Lead time	55	3	1.00	15
III. Qualitative				
a. Process	5	3	1.00	15
b. Basic R&D	2	0		0
c. Technology obsolescence	5	4	1.00	20
d. Product obsolescence	3	0		0
Total	100			250

analysis will be used to prepare time-phased cost analysis and return-on-investment projections for each project.

In the final summary of development and operating costs and benefits, it is generally desirable to describe each alternative at a consistent level of detail (including the "do-nothing" alternative) and in comparable terms. For example, the economic description of each specific project should include a complete presentation of the following:

- Development costs
- Quantifiable operating costs
- Other costs
- Relation of project to the strategic plan
- Tangible benefits
- Performance measures
- Intangible benefits (both measured and unmeasured)
- Risk factors
- Operating assumptions and constraints

Several lines of action are suggested for the proper measurement of benefits attained from implementing advanced manufacturing technologies.

Monitor Critical Costs and Performance Measures

At the conclusion of the initial cost-benefit analysis, develop a tracking plan that identifies the required information to be monitored, by success factors; the source of the "as-is" data; and the source of the "to-be" data. As advanced technology is incorporated into a manufacturing process, the type of information available from the process will change. The information required for the cost-benefit justification of the advanced technology should be evaluated relative to the information that is potentially available from the new process and from the present reporting system.

Ensure Compatibility with Standards

Cost and performance measures should be compatible with all internal and external requirements, including Generally Accepted Accounting Principles and cost accounting standards.

The cost-benefit tracking system should be structured to provide data from a common base that can be used to satisfy other compliance reporting requirements. One method of ensuring this result is to develop a matrix of benefit-tracking, operational-management, and financial-reporting requirements. Any data not currently being reported should be evaluated to determine whether they are at variance with good management concepts.

Collect Verifiable Data

The data provided by the cost-benefit tracking system must be verifiable and suitable for audit. Document all sources of information previously identified in the cost-benefit/cost-tracking plan, including report number (by date), person, or document number. Each assumption should be explained in detail, with supporting documentation where appropriate.

Track Results to Determine Whether Benefits Have Been Achieved

Cost-benefit projections should be tracked for a sufficient time to determine whether the actual savings have been achieved. Since most cost accounting systems are not structured on the same basis as capital-investment systems, an ongoing tracking of savings could best be achieved either by modifying the existing cost accounting system, developing a dual system, or performing a periodic review of the project results. The determination of whether to restructure the cost accounting system should be made relative to the perceived use of the information within the management decision-making process and the cost of modifying the system. Even if the decision is made to restructure the cost accounting system, the change should be evolutionary and integrated into the corporate strategic factory-modernization plan.

If the decision is made not to modify the current cost accounting system, periodic industrial engineering studies could be used to validate the savings. In this case, the cost-benefit tracking plan should include the timing and scope of the audits and the procedures used for verification of the results.

PROJECT CONTROL

An effective project-control system should ensure that progress to date is in line with the project plan; provide the latest estimate of the resources required to complete the project (forecast cost to complete); and confirm the viability of the product being developed.

Project Plan

Effective project control depends upon a comprehensive project plan, which breaks down the overall task into a series of individual stages, or milestones. The achievement of each milestone should be easy to identify and can be documented by a report, a drawing or design, or a decision. It will be necessary to allocate resources, such as people or materials, to each stage of the project. The usage of these resources will be built into the project plan, linked to the individual milestones. The satisfactory completion of each phase will therefore require not only that the end-product be made but also that the consumption of resources has not exceeded the amount allotted.

Each phase of the project will be broken down further into specific tasks, with responsibility for completion assigned to key individuals. It is only at this level that projects will be controlled properly.

If the end completion date is expected to change, or if the budgeted costs may be exceeded, this should be reported, so that possible corrective actions can be considered. In monitoring progress against the original project plan, it is also important to take into account at all times the likely final outcome.

There are several advantages to producing the reports. First, it is good discipline to consider the implications of past performance upon the future outcome of the project. If a potential problem can be identified at an early stage, it may still be possible to take corrective action. Second, forewarning of possible delays in one area may highlight adverse effects in another, related area. Finally, forecast overruns on one project may be offset against surpluses on another, thereby avoiding the need for undesirable reductions in the scope of the first project.

It should be emphasized that forecast reports can be used to full effect only if they are completed promptly, accurately, and frankly. As with any management report, late information is useless. Moreover, it is to the advantage of all concerned if likely deviations from plan are reported quickly and to their full extent. It is much better to know of a problem in advance than after the fact, when it might be too late to take action.

Product Viability Reports

The investment needed to develop a new product will have been justified by the expectation of increased profits and positive cash flows in the future. In most cases, there will be a time lag of several years before these benefits accrue. Many of the fundamental assumptions may have changed during this period, resulting in major variations in the financial returns. For example, sales volumes may have been reduced by the introduction of competitive products, or delays during the development phase may have delayed the introduction of the new product into the marketplace.

It is vital to bear in mind the future viability of the new product throughout its development. Despite the emotional consequences of canceling a major development project before it is complete, it is better to do so than to commit additional scarce resources to a "lost cause."

A periodic viability review may also bring to light understatements in benefits, which could themselves jeopardize the success of a product. For example, if customer demand has been underestimated, insufficient production capacity may be provided and sales will suffer because of long delays in meeting orders.

AN EXPERT SYSTEM FOR INVESTMENT JUSTIFICATION

This section describes an expert system developed by Major Steve LeClair of the United States Air Force to assist companies in the selection of advanced manufacturing technologies. CAM-I's CMS project served as one of the "experts" and provided a line of reasoning consistent with the conceptual design expressed in this chapter. The expert system will be tried out and evaluated by several CMS sponsors. Although it is still considered a research project, future enhancements could include refinement of the system based on a feedback loop, where the system would "learn" from reported actual performance of previous selections.

Figure 7.3 illustrates how decisions are made within the expert system in response to the user's responses. The arrows show the categories or items that support each decision. At the top center of the chart, for example, it is clear that advanced manufacturing technologies are matched with data about a user's top three concerns for improving manufacturing methods. If there is no match, the flow exits to the right and down, all the way to the no-go decision block.

If there is a match between the user's candidate technology and one of their top three improvement opportunity areas, the flow is down to the second decision point. There, the candidate technologies are matched against a list of technological prerequisites. If a prerequisite is found but it is not implemented, a decision to defer the project is recommended. Otherwise, the decision process continues. However, after a second decision point, additional informa-

Figure 7.3
Expert-System Model

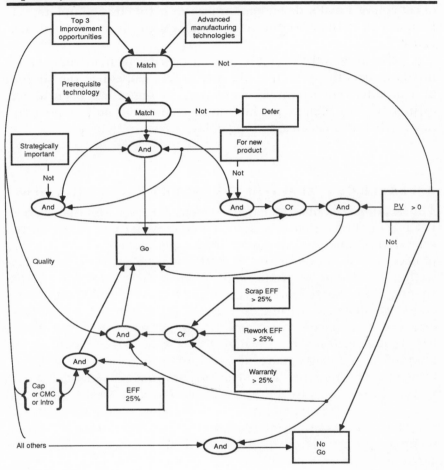

Source: Steve LeClair, U.S. Air Force.

tion is needed about the strategic importance of the technology; that is, whether it is necessary for the production of new products.

Figure 7.4 shows how advanced manufacturing technologies relate to specific opportunities to improve manufacturing methods. It is a matrix of specific kinds of technology versus specific manufacturing goals. The technologies are categorized by how they relate to

Figure 7.4
Advanced Manufacturing Technologies and Improved Opportunity Relations

	Inventory Reduction	Improved Space Utilization Layout & Material Flow	Decreased ECN'S	Reduced Shedule Changes	Improved Quality	Improved Standardization Of Parts & Products	Reduced Setups	Reduced Manufacturing	Reduced Product Introduction Cycle Time	Increased Capacity	Improved Information Timeliness & Documentation/Forecast Accuracy	Less Product Complexity
Design Focus												
Computer Aided Design			X		X							X
Computer Aided Engineering			X		X	X			X		X	
C.A. Testing/Simulation			X		X							
Computer Aided Process Planning	X	X	X		X	X	X	X	X	X		
Group Technology	X	X	X	X	X	X	X	X	X	X	X	X
Automated NC Programming Technology					X				X	X	X	
Design-To-Cost			X			X			X			X
Non Touch Focus												
Order Entry											X	
Capacity Planning	X	X		X				X		X	X	
Master Production Schedule				X						X	X	
MRP	X	X		X				X		X	X	
Inventory Management	X	X		X				X		X	X	
Factory Scheduling	X	X		X				X		X	X	
Shop Floor Control	X	X		X				X		X	X	
Other Manufacturing Planning & Control Projects	X	X		X				X		X	X	
Touch Focus												
Robotics					X						X	
Computer Aided Machining (NC/CNC)	X	X			X		X	X			X	
Computer Aided Inspection					X						X	
Automated Material Handling	X	X			X			X			X	
FMS	X	X		X	X		X	X			X	
Specialized Equipment					X		X	X			X	
Process Specific Projects	X	X			X			X			X	
Other/Multi												
Total Quality Control					X							X
JIT	X	X		X	X	X	X	X		X		X
Electronic Links To Supplier/Customer	X	X			X			X			X	
Pull Production	X	X		X	X							
Integration	X	X		X	X		X	X	X	X	X	

Source: Steve LeClair, U.S. Air Force.

specific kinds of activities. Complementary data points make the expert system at once robust and specific: the more data the system has, the more accurate its decisions can be.

The expert system described here is not intended to provide absolute answers but to provide investment justification guidance, using principles similar to those used by managers familiar with manufacturing investment decisions. The CAM-I CMS provides this expert system to illustrate both the intricacy of the investment justification process and the significant contribution that expert systems can make to sound investment management.

FURTHER READINGS

Firmin, P. A., and J. J. Linn. "Information Systems and Managerial Accounting." *The Accounting Review* (January 1968): 75–82.

Haseman, W. D., and A. B. Whinston. "Design of a Multidimensional Accounting System." *The Accounting Review* (January 1976): 65–79.

Hayes, R. H., and S. C. Wheelwright. "The Dynamics of Process-Product Life Cycles." *Harvard Business Review* (March–April 1979): 127–136.

Kaplan, R. S. "Measuring Manufacturing Performance: A New Challenge for Managerial Accounting Research." *The Accounting Review* (October 1983): 686–704.

Lucas, H. C. "The Use of an Accounting Information System, Action, and Organizational Performance." *The Accounting Review* (October 1975): 735–746.

Richardson, P. R., and J. R. M. Gordon. "Measuring Total Manufacturing Performance." *Sloan Management Review* (Winter 1980): 47–58.

Skinner, W. "Manufacturing—Missing Link in Corporate Strategy." *Harvard Business Review* (May–June 1969): 136–145.

———. "The Focused Factory." *Harvard Business Review* (May–June 1974): 114–121.

Williams, J. R. "Schumpeterian Economics of Scope." Working paper, Graduate School of Industrial Administration, Carnegie-Mellon University, June 1983.

CHAPTER 8

Issues of Cost Management in Relation to the Cost Accounting Standards (CAS)

T his chapter discusses the issues of cost management for government contractors in the light of existing cost accounting standards. The cost accounting practices used in performance of government contracts must comply with the requirements of the Cost Accounting Standards (CAS). This chapter discusses the CAS requirements, identifies potential problem areas that may surface during the transition to a CIM environment, and provides recommendations as to how these problems can be addressed most constructively.

The content of this chapter reflects the general consensus of the group but does not necessarily represent the opinion of any one of the individual participants or the official position of their respective organizations.

OVERVIEW

The introduction of automated equipment into the manufacturing environment, coupled with the increased ability to handle data, creates a great opportunity to better measure, report, and control costs. If costs are more discretely linked with the factors that cause them or with the products they benefit, management is better able to make decisions on utilizing available resources effectively. The implementation of more precise cost accounting enhances the cost efficiency of operations.

It has been alleged that the CAS will greatly impede, if not entirely preclude, the introduction of significant accounting revisions designed to measure, accumulate, and report costs more directly in a manner compatible with an automated environment. We do not believe that the CAS precludes these accounting revisions. In fact, specific identification to the maximum extent practical is totally consonant with the fundamental cost-allocation hierarchy that underlies all the standards.

However, there are pitfalls that could waylay unsuspecting managers and impede progress toward the establishment of computer-aided manufacturing processes. Our primary objective is to help people avoid or at least efficiently administer difficult issues through the identification of potential problem areas and the offering of recommended approaches toward resolution.

In a general sense, the CAS implications are twofold. First, managers must consider the CAS rules regarding the implementation of "accounting changes." Second, the compliance with applicable, individual standards must be evaluated. This chapter addresses both implications, using terms common to (and formally defined in) the various CAS promulgations. Also included is a checklist designed to assist managers by highlighting important considerations that should be evaluated prior to putting new cost management systems and accounting practices in place.

COST ACCOUNTING CHANGES

The introduction of highly automated manufacturing processes and attendant cost management systems can result in concurrent revisions to existing cost accounting practices. While changes to cost accounting practices are permitted under the CAS Clause, Federal Acquisition Regulation 52.230-3, the financial impact on current CAS-covered contracts can vary depending upon the circumstances. Therefore, the administration of cost accounting changes is a subject that warrants prospective analysis as companies move toward the implementation of the factory of the future. This topic can be divided logically into two parts: (1) applicability of the CAS Clause, and (2) administration of the CAS Clause accounting-change provisions.

Clearly, the administration of the specific provisions of the CAS Clause only becomes relevant after it has been determined that the CAS Clause is in fact applicable to the accounting revision in question. It should be noted at the outset that the circumstances surrounding the introduction of automated processes will differ from location to location. It is impractical to discuss every conceivable situation. Consequently, this chapter focuses on basic concepts as potential problem areas.

Applicability of the CAS Clause

The provisions of the CAS Clause are applicable to changes made to cost accounting practices. On March 10, 1978, the Cost Accounting Standards Board (CASB) promulgated a formal definition of a "cost accounting practice" and a "change" thereto. Specifically, 4 CFR 331.20(k) defines a "cost accounting practice" as ". . . any disclosed or established accounting method or technique which is used for measurement of cost, assignment of cost to cost accounting periods, or allocation of cost to cost objectives." Per 4 CFR 331.20(l), a cost accounting "change" is any "alteration" in a cost accounting practice *except* (i) the initial adoption of a cost accounting practice for the first time a cost is incurred or a function is created, and (ii) a revision of a practice that had previously been immaterial in amount.

Before we specifically address the application of these definitions in connection with the transition to automated facilities or processes, some general observations are worth noting.

The CASB's prefatory comments to 4 CFR 331.20 discuss the proposition that the cause or motivation underlying a revision to current practices should be determinative with respect to the applicability of the CAS Clause. Opinions were expressed that revisions resulting from changed circumstances or from the issuance of new regulations or laws should not be subject to the CAS Clause. The CASB clearly rejected these opinions and concluded that the reason for implementing a change is irrelevant in this regard. If a revision qualifies as a "change" to a "cost accounting practice," the CAS Clause is applicable regardless of the reason for its adoption. As discussed later, the reason underlying a cost accounting change *is* pertinent with respect to the treatment accorded a change under the CAS Clause.

Notwithstanding the definition given in 4 CFR 331.20, determining what constitutes a "cost accounting practice" can be difficult. Cost accounting practices may be general methodologies (e.g., method of establishing asset service lives) or specific, clear-cut procedures (e.g., amortization period for actuarial gains and losses). Each circumstance must be individually evaluated. It is often helpful to examine the illustrations set forth in 4 CFR 331.20(j) and to attempt to draw meaningful parallels. Similar problems exist in connection with the exception in 4 CFR 331.20(l)(1). An initial adoption of a cost accounting practice does not qualify as a "cost accounting change." However, this exception is limited in scope to those instances where a new cost is incurred or a new function is created. Unfortunately, when plant operations are altered, the nature of the resources expended often changes, and the related costs change form (e.g., from labor to depreciation). It is frequently difficult to distinguish between a new cost element and a different form of an existing cost element.

Focusing on the functions being performed both before and after the implementation of revised operations is normally the most productive analytical approach. Except for externally imposed costs (e.g., a new state tax), rarely is a new cost incurred in the absence of the concurrent undertaking of a new function. Again, drawing parallels with the illustrations in 4 CFR 331.20(j) can help guide such decisions.

Automation and Cost Accounting Changes. With regard to introducing advanced manufacturing technology, managers will be confronted with a variety of accounting-change issues. Substituting automated processes for existing labor-oriented processes will raise questions concerning creation, deletion, and retention of functions. The CASB's publications do not expressly define "function." However, the illustrations in 4 CFR 331.20(m)(3) shed some light on this subject. For example, accounting revisions related to the initial offering of retirement benefits or the termination of a segment and its nuclear-energy research effort do not qualify as cost accounting changes. Here are two examples that illustrate the foregoing points.

Situation A. A company operates a labor-intensive pipe-bending process. Computer-aided machinery is introduced to perform the same process. The manufacturing overhead allocation basis is changed from direct-labor hours to machine hours.

Situation B. A company operates a labor-intensive pipe-bending process. Computer-aided machinery is introduced to perform the same process. Concurrently, a semi-automated metal-chroming process is added to the company's manufacturing operation. Two manufacturing overhead pools are established. The pipe-bending overhead allocation basis is changed from direct-labor hours to machine hours. The metal-chroming overhead is distributed on a unit-of-output basis.

In situation A it would appear that the existing function remains intact. Only the *form* of the resources expended in the performance of the function has changed. Consequently, the change in allocation basis represents a cost accounting change. While the same conclusion can be reached with respect to the pipe-bending process in situation B, the metal-chroming operation appears to be a new function, and the addition of a new overhead pool and a new allocation basis may well fall within the exception in 4 CFR 331.20(l)(1).

As another example, assume that a company decides to build an entirely new facility that is a separate segment with different disclosed practices. Manufacturing of some subitems required in the performance of existing contracts are transferred to this new segment. Is a cost accounting involved? From one perspective, a cost accounting change has occurred, since no new function has been created. The existing function remains unaltered. On the other hand, this situation could be likened to a change in a make/buy decision, which typically has not been classified as a cost accounting change. Pursuit of an advance agreement (FAR 31.109) between the company and the government detailing the application or non-application of the CAS Clause is recommended.

The depreciation of computer-aided machinery will require significant evaluation. Consider the situation of a company that invests heavily, and for the first time, in robotics. The company currently depreciates factory equipment (the asset accountability unit) on a straight-line basis over an asset service life of ten years. It also depreciates new equipment (in which it has no prior experience) over a service life based on the midpoint of the Internal Revenue Service (IRS) guidelines until adequate historical data are developed. The company establishes a new asset accountability unit, with a five-year (presumed IRS midpoint) useful life, to be depreciated on an accelerated basis.

The illustration in 4 CFR 331.20(m)(3) suggests that the adoption of the five-year service life corresponds to the company's current practice. But the accelerated depreciation practice represents either the initial adoption of an accounting practice for the first time a cost is incurred (i.e., cost of a new type of machinery), or a "change" (per CAS) in the manner in which existing cost (equipment depreciation) is measured. In the past, the government has taken the latter position with regard to the adoption of revised billing methods necessitated by the introduction of new computer systems.

CAS Clause Accounting-Change Provisions

Contractual actions that result from applying the provisions of the CAS Clause to cost accounting changes depend on how the changes are classified. The CAS Clause establishes three different classes of cost accounting changes: mandatory, voluntary, and mutually agreed-to voluntary.

Mandatory changes encompass those changes necessitated by the promulgation of a new cost accounting standard or the initial application of existing standards (e.g., when a contractor receives its first CAS-covered contract). Equitable adjustments reflecting the cost impact on existing CAS-covered contracts are required.

Voluntary changes are all changes other than mandatory ones. Unless mutually agreed-to by the cognizant government contracting officer, any increased cost to existing CAS-covered contracts must be disallowed. This exclusion applies to *aggregate* increases: that is, offsets (increases versus decreases) between individual contracts are permitted—it is the net that is disallowed (if it is an increase).

Mutually agreed-to changes are voluntary changes where the cognizant government contracting officer determines that the change is beneficial and not detrimental to the government's interest. In such cases, equitable adjustments reflecting the cost impact are permitted, regardless of the nature (increase or decrease) of the net aggregate impact on all CAS-covered contracts.

It is unlikely that any of the cost accounting changes precipitated by the introduction of computer-aided equipment will be mandatory in nature. Admittedly, to the extent that the new technology allows for more discrete identification of cost elements to final cost objectives, the direct charging of these expenses may be required in order to remain in compliance with CAS 418. Nevertheless, cost accounting revisions needed to stay in compliance with an existing standard are technically voluntary changes for CAS purposes. Most, if not all, of these cost accounting changes will be voluntary or mutually agreed-to changes. Some circumstances will involve a combination of both types of changes, necessitating a separate analysis for each individual change.

Government contracting officers have a great deal of discretionary authority in determining whether a change should be mutually agreed-to. DOD Working Group Paper No. 79-23 expressly states that the projected cost impact on existing CAS-covered contracts is not the only criterion: appropriateness or equity of the change and the impact on future contracts are also factors to be considered. Naturally, if it is projected that there will be a negative impact on existing CAS-covered contracts, a strong rationale addressing the appropriateness of the revised accounting practice must be present to support mutual agreement. In addition, the future benefits in terms of future increased productivity, enhanced quality, and so on, should be detailed and quantified to the maximum extent possible.

On the surface, the lack of mutual agreement between contractor and government would appear to forebode serious financial consequences, given a front-loaded endeavor like the introduction of automated equipment. The aggregate cost charged to existing CAS-covered contracts may well increase, with the contractor having to absorb this increase out of profit.

However, there are frequently two mitigating factors in such cases. First, cost offsets (increases and decreases) are permitted among individual, voluntary cost accounting changes that are simultaneously implemented. Second, and more important, it is necessary to distinguish between cost impact related to the change in *accounting practices* and cost impact related to the change in *machinery* or *equipment*.

The introduction of new equipment will undoubtedly increase facility-related costs (depreciation, utilities) regardless of whether there are concurrent cost accounting changes. This increase in costs is *not* a component of the CAS cost impact. For CAS purposes, the cost impact is limited to the change in costs charged to CAS-covered contracts due to a revision in cost measurement, assignment, or allocation.

This segregation is not an easy task. On the other hand, it has been successfully performed in the past when new computer systems were introduced. The key is the establishment of a consistent baseline. Given a constant expenditure level, what is the cost charged to existing CAS-covered contracts under the new accounting practices versus the old ones? Advance planning and coordination are imperative if agreement on the CAS cost impact is to be reached in a timely manner.

COMPLIANCE WITH INDIVIDUAL STANDARDS
Planning and Disclosure

Before the changed practices are actually implemented, it is necessary to submit an "adequate disclosure" of the changed practices and to consider their compliance with the individual standards. Special note should be made of the disclosure requirements. "Adequate disclosure" means that the description of the new practice must be *current, accurate,* and *complete.* This requirement is a precondition to contracting with the government and should be accomplished as far as possible in advance of implementation. Submission of a revised disclosure statement should be a manufacturer's top priority to allow sufficient time for government review and the resolution of issues before implementation.

Unlike adequate disclosure, compliance with the individual standards should not affect the ability to contract. But, again, advance resolution of compliance questions can significantly reduce the overall administrative effort. It is far easier to change a plan than to change an accounting system once it has been put in place.

Another advantage of satisfying the disclosure requirement well in advance of implementation is the reduction in the number of contracts potentially subject to adjustment. The greater the lead time between adequate disclosure of new compliant practices and implementation of the new practices, the larger the number of existing contracts priced in accordance with the new accounting practices. These contracts do not need to be adjusted and may be deleted from the cost-impact statement.

CAS 401. Consistency in Estimating, Accumulating, and Reporting Costs

This standard requires consistency in a contractor's method of estimating costs for a proposal and the method used to accumulate and report actual costs under a contract.

Forward-pricing problems can surface when an accounting system is changed to permit more discrete identification, accumulation, and allocation of costs. Extensive changes of this type can destroy the ability to utilize historical data as a basis for estimating future costs. This can precipitate initial cost proposals for work to be performed in an automated factory that could run far afield of actual cost. And yet, once the new accounting practices have been adequately disclosed and implemented, CAS 401 requires that cost proposals be consistent with these disclosed practices. (Also, see FAR 15.804, which addresses the submittal of cost and pricing data.)

FAR 31.109. Advance Agreements Addressing Forward Pricing. It is recommended that the contractor consummate FAR 31.109 advance agreements addressing how forward pricing is to be handled. One alternative is to construct and agree upon an accounting model based on reasonable assumptions, which will provide a foundation for initially estimating future costs and for measuring the cost impact on current government contracts. The development of assumptions in which both contractor and government have an acceptable degree of confidence can be difficult but is possible in some situations.

Another option is to run dual accounting systems (old and new practices) for a specified period. While expensive, this approach allows for the validation of the new accounting software; lets the parties agree to continue pricing and costing the old way until cost data under the new accounting practices are developed; and provides an excellent baseline for measuring the cost impact.

CAS 402. Consistency in Allocating Costs Incurred for the Same Purpose

CAS 402 requires that costs incurred for the same purpose under like circumstances be charged direct only or indirect only to all final cost objectives.

During the transition to a CIM facility, there may be one or more islands of automation within an existing business segment. Because of the increased capability of computer-aided machinery to identify costs specifically to the individual parts being processed, concurrent direct and indirect charging of like costs (e.g., depreciation) can result. This situation will probably precipitate CAS 402 noncompliance allegations. While it might be argued that the enhanced capability to identify costs specifically constitutes an unlike circumstance, it may be difficult to reach mutual agreement on this point.

Double-Charging. Nevertheless, this apparent dilemma can be overcome. The key to an administrative resolution is the avoidance of double-charging. In the absence of double-charging, there is rarely a significant cost impact associated with the alleged CAS 402 violation. At worst, the contractor is normally confronted with "technical noncompliance" and an administrative resolution is obtainable.

How is double-charging to be avoided in this environment? The answer lies in the tracking of the flow of parts or units of output through the various manufacturing processes. For example, assume it is practical to charge directly the depreciation of a computer-aided pipe-bending machine to the parts passing through it. All of the remaining plant or equipment depreciation is recovered through overhead. As long as all the parts being produced in the plant pass through this automated pipe-bending process and receive a direct charge, there is no double-charging. However, if there is a mixture of parts, some of which do not require pipe-bending, then care must be taken to ensure that the parts subject to the automated process do not receive an indirect allocation of depreciation related to other equipment not used in their production.

CAS 403. Allocation of Home-Office Expenses to Segments

At many locations CAS 403 requires that residual expenses be distributed to segments via a prescribed three-factor formula (payroll, capital, and property). Be aware that the factory of the future may not draw an equitable share of residual home-office expenses if a contractor allocates such expenses using the three-factor formula. This results from the low amount of payroll dollars in the automated factory. Any skewing may be offset, however, by indicating a larger percentage of tangible capital assets.

Residual-Pool Composition. Major concerns in this area can be avoided as long as the residual pool is kept to a minimum. Thus, when exploring the impact on a three-factor formula allocation basis, one should also review the composition of the residual pool to see if there are any cost elements that can be deleted from the residual pool and allocated to segments on a more discrete basis.

Surrogate Bases for Residual Expenses. At those locations where the three-factor formula is not applied, the residual costs are allocated to segments on a surrogate basis that adequately represents total activity. Head count, gross payroll, and other labor-oriented bases are commonly used in this regard. When automation is introduced, the labor content of total cost can be reduced drastically. The continued viability of these bases should be evaluated.

CAS 404. Capitalization of Tangible Assets

The cost of developing or purchasing the computer software necessary to run an automated facility will be significant. Most software costs currently are expensed. However, the cost of software that interconnects, communicates, and substantially controls the automated factory will be significant and may be subject to a capitalization challenge.

Computer-Software Costs. Specifically, CAS 404 requires capitalization of "costs necessary to prepare the asset for use," including the costs of "bringing the asset to a condition necessary for normal or expected use." In addition, "all indirect costs properly allocable" to constructed or fabricated assets are capitalized. An argument *against* capitalization is that software is not a tangible asset—it fails to meet the definition set forth in CAS 404.30(a)(4)—and capitalization of the related development cost raises the complex issues of treatment of major software revisions and application of CAS 414/417.

It is recommended that consideration be given to including the cost of software, integral to the performance of computer-aided machinery, in the capitalized value of that equipment. This accounting approach recognizes the extended service life of the software; provides a better matching of period costs with resource consumption; and substantially reduces current-period rate increases due to the significant startup costs associated with the introduction of automation.

Financial Accounting. It should be noted that this approach, in conjunction with in-house developed software, may be contrary to policies adopted under Generally Accepted Accounting Principles (GAAP) and thus may conflict with a company's existing financial accounting practices. It is recommended that the issue of capitalizing versus expensing software costs be elevated to the attention of appropriate DOD policy representatives. The current rules and regulations are deficient and do not adequately address this significant cost element.

CAS 407. Use of Standard Costs for Direct Material and Direct Labor

CAS 407 contains criteria for the establishment and accumulation of direct labor and material standards and the accumulation and disposition of variances. The *production unit* is the appropriate level for establishing standards and accumulating variances. Variances are allocated annually on the basis of the cost the standard was set to measure. (Immaterial variances may be included in indirect cost pools.)

CAS 407 permits the use of standard costs only if variances are accounted for at the production-unit (product-line) level. Recovery of variances booked to cost-of-sales as a period expense is prohibited.

Labor rate and time standards probably will not be set for an automated factory because of the decline in direct labor. Labor costs will be incurred to support and maintain the automated facility, but these charges may not represent direct labor.

The introduction of increased automation may lead to more widespread use of standard cost systems and, therefore, increased application of CAS 407. This standard does not expressly discuss the establishment of machine-hour or process standards that are likely to be used in an automated manufacturing facility. Nevertheless, it is recommended that the contractor assume that similar accounting principles apply. It is also recommended that the lack of express coverage of machine-hour or process standards be brought to the attention of appropriate DOD policy representatives.

CAS 409. Depreciation of Tangible Capital Assets

As factories become more automated, equipment cost will increase significantly. This standard requires that equipment be depreciated over an estimated service life that reflects its expected period of usefulness. The estimated service life must be supported by previous experience with similar assets. The machinery in an automated factory is leading-edge, and hence there will be limited or no experience with similar assets. Lacking such experience, what should the contractor do?

Equipment Not Covered by an IRS ADR Class. In such cases, the standard allows write-offs over the expected actual period of usefulness, but not less than the IRS ADR midpoint. Because the IRS has not established a relevant ADR midpoint for robotic equipment, it is recommended that a FAR 31.109 advance agreement be pursued to cover a mutually agreed-to service life.

Direct Charging of Depreciation Costs. CAS 409 permits the direct charging of depreciation, *provided these charges are allocated based on usage and all similar equipment depreciation is charged in the same manner* (see also CAS 402). In instances where the automated facilities can allocate costs and maintain time on the usage directly related to a product, these costs should be charged directly to the product. This approach is contrary to current accounting practices, where the facilities depreciation is normally an indirect cost charged to overhead. The equipment might be placed in a service center with an estimated usage rate that would allocate costs to departments using the automated equipment. The distinction is whether the facilities are automated to the point where costs and time can be measured by that specific facility.

Technological Change and the Allocation of Depreciation Costs. The prospect of rapidly changing technology raises concerns over the continued use of traditional depreciation methods to assign equipment costs to accounting periods. The opinion has been expressed that automated machinery depreciation cost should be measured and assigned to accounting periods on the basis of usage.

To illustrate, consider the following example: A piece of computer-aided machinery has a capitalized value of $1,000. It is anticipated that the machine is capable of producing 1,000 units before requiring replacement. During the machine's service life, one dollar of depreciation cost would be recorded as each unit is produced. If the machine is rendered technologically obsolete after producing only 750 units, the remaining unabsorbed depreciation cost of $250 would be recorded in an overhead account and charged (indirectly) to final cost objectives in the period in which the asset is retired.

The assignment of depreciation cost to accounting periods on the basis of usage appears to agree with the resource-consumption concept in CAS 409. On the other hand, there are a couple of potential problem areas associated with this approach. First, the suggested recovery of unabsorbed cost through overhead probably will raise CAS 409 compliance questions. Second, this depreciation method will complicate forward-pricing efforts. The contractor and government will have to reach a mutual agreement not only on the total estimated usage of the machine but also on the anticipated timing of the usage over several accounting records. These factors should be evaluated carefully and discussed before adoption of this methodology is proposed formally.

CAS 410. Allocation of Business Unit General and Administrative Expenses to Final Cost Objectives

General and administrative (G&A) expenses must be allocated to final cost objectives on the cost-input allocation basis that best represents the total activity of the business unit. Depending upon the circumstances, the basis selected may be total cost input, value added, or a single element (direct-labor dollars, direct-labor hours).

As computer-aided technology is introduced into a manufacturing facility, the ratio of direct-labor cost to total cost is likely to decrease substantially. The continued appropriateness of the existing G&A allocation base should then be examined. This is especially true with respect to single-element bases such as direct-labor hours or direct-labor dollars. As labor becomes a smaller component of total cost, questions will probably surface as to whether such bases still best represent "total activity." At some point, it could be that some other cost-input basis (total cost input, machine hours) will be more appropriate.

CAS 414. Cost of Money as an Element of the Cost of Facilities Capital

CAS 417. Cost of Money as an Element of the Cost of Capital Assets under Construction

CAS 414 and 417 establish criteria for measuring and allocating the cost of facilities capital. The standards, along with the Federal Acquisition Regulations, permit a contractor to claim cost of money (COM), based on a Treasury rate, as an allowable contract cost. The CASB wished to encourage contractors' investments in modern facilities and recognized that a fair return on capital assets is a normal business cost. COM is an important consideration when companies are contemplating significant investments in automated factory equipment and the introduction of advanced technologies.

Recovery of COM Associated with CIM-Software Investment. Some strong arguments can be made to allow COM on the computer-software investment for automated manufacturing. However, arguing for COM supports recognition of software costs as a capital asset subject to depreciation. Consistent with our recommendation about CAS 404, it is suggested that software forming an integral part of the automated equipment be included in both the capitalized value of the equipment and in COM computations.

CAS 418. Allocation of Direct and Indirect Costs

This standard requires the establishment of homogeneous indirect-cost pools, with the cost of all activities in a single pool having the same causal/beneficial relation to final cost objectives. Each indirect-cost pool must be allocated on a basis that reflects the causal/beneficial relation. This fundamental concept parallels the general thrust of advanced CMS models, which call for more discrete identification of cost with cost objectives.

Direct-labor Allocation Bases. Traditional allocation bases (e.g., direct labor) should be reviewed when establishing automated facilities. It may be inappropriate to allocate a pool of costs on a direct-labor cost or hour basis in an automated environment. A direct-labor basis may not represent the true causal/beneficial relation, and cost objectives may not receive a fair share of cost. Utilization of a usage basis, such as units of output or machine hours, may be a better alternative.

Progressive Changes. The typical scenario is a gradual phasing-in of automation, progressing from no automation through islands of automation to integrated automation. As a contractor's manufacturing methods change, so will accounting practices. This logically would lead to a series of individual accounting changes. Such a progression can involve continual government review, large accounting changes, auditing expenses, and lengthy delays.

To preclude this, consideration should be given to amending the disclosure statement *in advance* and including the criteria that will be applied to determine if and when a change from a direct-labor to a usage allocation basis is appropriate. Then, as computer-aided machinery is acquired, and changes in allocation basis are implemented per the disclosed criteria, no disclosure statement change is required.

Compliance with CAS 401. Note that CAS 401 problems can develop if these changes in allocation basis are not foreseen and contracts are not priced accordingly. Estimating overhead on a direct-labor basis and subsequently costing the same overhead on a machine-hour basis constitutes an inconsistency that is not permitted by CAS 401.

Startup Expenses and Allocation Problems. Any time there are significant startup costs in connection with automated facilities, allocation of these costs on a usage basis can present a problem when only a small portion of the business initially uses the facilities. Industry practice has been to expense an appropriate portion of startup costs, including depreciation, to a plantwide overhead account; capitalize all such costs and amortize them over projected service life; or absorb part of the costs as a company-sponsored venture. It is recommended that the proposed practice be discussed well in advance with the government representative. A FAR 31.109 advance agreement should be pursued.

The issue of equitable cost recovery involving high-cost facilities with small or even nonexistent business volume is not limited to the factory of the future. The same issue frequently surfaces in connection with test and other special-purpose facilities. It was just this problem that led to the "special facilities" exemption set forth in CAS 418.50(f). It is recommended that the issue of high-cost, low-volume facilities be brought to the attention of the appropriate DOD policy authority.

CAS 420. Accounting for Independent Research and Development Cost and Bid and Proposal Costs

Independent research and development (IR&D) costs and bid and proposal (B&P) costs must be allocated to final cost objectives on a basis that reflects the causal/beneficial relation. Generally, IR&D/B&P will be allocated on the same basis as G&A expense.

As previously discussed in connection with CAS 410, the introduction of automation could affect the continued viability of some G&A allocation bases. Since IR&D/B&P is commonly distributed on the same basis as G&A cost, a change in G&A basis could precipitate a change in the way IR&D/B&P is allocated. This is another potential issue that contractors should be aware of during the transition to the factory of the future.

SUMMARY

The implementation and administration of a cost accounting change can be an arduous and controversial procedure. However, if approached in a proactive mode, the administrative workload and adverse financial impact on current programs can be substantially reduced. Advance planning, coordination, and review are the keys. The further in advance of implementation a revised disclosure statement is submitted, reviewed, and agreed-to, the smaller the number of contracts subject to adjustment. Also, advance agreement on the methodology to be used in developing the cost impact and complying with the standards is desirable.

The following points summarize the foregoing discussion of government contracting and automation-induced cost accounting revisions:

1. The cause or motivation underlying an accounting revision is not germane to the determination of whether the revision

qualifies as a cost accounting change but is relevant in determining its treatment as a mutually agreed-to versus purely voluntary change.

2. Comparing the functions being performed both before and after the accounting revision is usually the most productive analytical approach to determining whether an accounting revision constitutes a cost accounting change.

3. Treatment as a mutually agreed-to, voluntary accounting change depends not only on the estimated cost impact on existing contracts but also on the appropriateness of the new accounting practice and the potential downstream benefits associated with the automated processes underlying the revised practice.

4. The cost impact associated with a cost accounting change is limited solely to the difference in costs charged to CAS-covered contracts due to the change in cost measurement, assignment, and allocation. The change in total cost incurred due to the introduction of new machinery and the reduction of labor resources are not part of the CAS cost-impact assessment.

5. When confronted with significant changes, the running of dual accounting systems, for a limited period, could facilitate forward-pricing and cost-impact calculations.

6. The anticipated treatment to be accorded software should be the topic of advance discussion and agreement. Inclusion of the related software cost in the capitalized value of the automated equipment is the recommended approach. However, the overall issue of software accounting should be discussed with DOD policy officials.

7. The fact that CAS 407 does not expressly address machine-hour or usage standards should be brought to the attention of the appropriate DOD policy officials. It is recommended that accounting principles similar to those required by CAS 407 in connection with direct labor and material be applied to machine-hour standards.

8. Since the IRS has not established a relevant ADR midpoint for robotic equipment, a FAR 31.109 advance agreement that establishes a mutually agreed-to asset service life should be pursued.

9. When practical, the depreciation in connection with automated

equipment should be directly charged to the product. Care must be taken to ensure that this same product does not concurrently receive an indirect allocation of depreciation associated with similar equipment.

10. Because of the rapid advance of technology, consideration should be given to assigning the depreciation cost of automated equipment on a usage or resource-consumption basis.

11. As the ratio of direct labor to total cost diminishes, serious consideration should be given to adopting a usage allocation basis, such as units of output or machine hours.

12. The issue of recovery of startup costs associated with an automated facility should be reviewed in advance, and the consummation of a FAR 31.109 advance agreement should be considered.

Following is a management checklist of important considerations that should be taken into account during the management-planning process.

1. Consider timing of implementation to avoid repricing current contracts, and minimize the cost impact (whether building new advanced manufacturing facilities or introducing CAD/CAM to current manufacturing facilities).

2. Determine functions/costs that are being added and that therefore do *not* represent cost accounting changes.

3. Determine which costs will increase or decrease significantly (e.g., labor and depreciation) but will not change with respect to how they are measured, allocated, or assigned to periods.

4. List the true, proposed cost accounting changes, omitting items identified under (2) and (3).

5. Identify the rationale for the proposed changes. Consider the implications of the proposed changes in establishing precedents for the future.

6. Analyze the rationale for each change, and question whether the same justification could be applied to other CAS-covered operations within the company. In other words, if the changes are beneficial in a CIM environment because they result in a more appropriate allocation of costs, should those same changes be made elsewhere in the company?

7. If the situation represents a transition from a traditional factory

to a fully automated facility, consider making all of the proposed cost accounting changes at the same time to benefit from offsets.

8. Document the impact of the automation on the ability to meet future contract needs. Include savings from labor costs, productivity improvements, and quality.

9. Consider the impact of the automation on other rates, even if there is no cost accounting change. For example, the related decrease in labor costs may shift costs that are allocated based on gross payroll to other operations.

10. Consider the appropriateness of separately disclosing an advanced manufacturing facility.

11. Analyze the implications of capitalizing some or all of the software costs related to the manufacturing process. Any policy on capitalizing software must be definitive enough to preclude ex post facto application.

CHAPTER 9

Cost Accounting in Japan

C AM-I representatives traveled to Japan in the fall of 1986 to study cost management in Japanese industries in order to understand Japanese cost accounting practices; to identify trends of change in these practices; and to explore the significance of any observed differences between Japanese and Western accounting methods. This chapter discusses the findings of the team: just as in America and Europe, existing management accounting methods do not adequately depict and measure strategic issues.

First, it is important to state some of the limitations of the study. None of the team members were experts on Japanese culture or language. The sample was neither random nor scientifically controlled: the team interviewed a small sample of industrial companies, accounting firms, consulting organizations, and academies.* No small companies were selected for interviews. Therefore, the observations presented here are somewhat impressionistic and may not be representative of Japanese management as a whole.

Furthermore, it is difficult to generalize about a complex environment, where accounting practices are intertwined with the social and political environment. Also, because of language problems, different interpretations of terms may have led to less-than-complete understanding of the Japanese practices or of the foundation that supports those practices.

Despite these limitations, however, the team reported these significant differences between Japanese cost management and the concepts presented in this book:

- Japanese cost management is guided by the concept of target cost. That is, management decides, before the product is designed,

---

* The names of the companies and individuals interviewed are listed at the end of this chapter.

what a product should cost, based on marketing (rather than manufacturing) factors.

- Cost planning and cost reduction receive more emphasis in Japanese companies than does cost control.
- Investment decisions are guided more by companywide agreement on cost/performance goals than by the financial justification favored in Western companies.

JAPANESE PHILOSOPHY OF COST MANAGEMENT

At least partly because of sociocultural issues, the general Japanese philosophy of cost management emphasizes a company's holistic approach to management in general and to cost planning and cost reduction in particular. This is different from Western methods, which are dedicated to cost control of specialized units.

Personnel Issues

The cost management ramifications of the Japanese practice (in larger companies) of lifetime employment are a strong emphasis on improved productivity and the reduction of labor costs. Participating employees reduce labor costs for a given product by moving labor where it is most needed (e.g., to new or growing product lines). This allows companies to fulfill the promise of guaranteed employment without fixing labor costs (on a product-by-product basis).

In addition, Japanese management tends to take a long-term view of investment justification and seeks a plantwide consensus of all levels on technology issues. These combine to provide a consistent, stable view of growth while enhancing individual workers' view of their value to the company.

The Japanese commitment to job rotation is also important. During managers' initial ten to fifteen years' employment with a given company, they work in manufacturing, accounting, engineering, and other areas, generally spending about three to four years in each. This creates a broad knowledge and appreciation of cost among management, engineering, and manufacturing personnel. It means that most managers have detailed knowledge of cost factors and practices.

Japanese worker compensation includes a base salary plus bonus.

The bonuses are paid twice yearly and equal two or three months' salary. However, unlike management-by-objective (MBO) incentives, the Japanese bonuses relate to *company* rather than *individual* performance. This practice has a significant effect on performance measurement.

Relative Importance of Costs

The Japanese commitment to lifetime employment, coupled with a limited internal marketplace, has dictated a national emphasis on growth, increased market share (dominance), flexibility, and meeting customers' needs. However, achievement of these goals does not preclude the emphasis on achieving profit. The primary goal of Japanese companies, as with Western organizations, is profit. Differences lie in the methods employed for achieving profits: the Japanese emphasize increased market share as the key to profitability. In addition, the role of physical measures (cycle time, meeting production schedules, defect rates, innovation) is important in the Japanese cost management philosophy. Japanese managers believe that improvements in physical measures will lead to greater long-term profits. This appears to de-emphasize the importance of formal cost control as an issue in manufacturing. In reality, it represents a different form of control, with the final objective still being increased profitability. For example, it is clear that managers who understand the cost behavior of all phases of product development and production will be more likely to lead profitable, well-run companies.

Importance of Long-Term Perspectives

Michiharu Sakurai, professor of accounting at Senshu University in Tokyo, attributed Japanese methods of capital investment to the long-term perspective of Japanese companies. The national emphasis on long-term performance has had a strong influence on management. This far-sighted approach is in direct contrast to U.S. methods, wherein stockholder earnings per share receive a large part of management attention. In Japan it is not clear how company performance is measured, who measures it, and how or to whom it is reported. Japanese companies, for example, are not required to issue quarterly financial reports to stockholders. CEOs and COOs are very rarely replaced at Japanese companies. In some cases, where firms have borrowed heavily, banks are involved with the company and clearly measure its performance.

Emphasis on Target Cost Results in Cost Reduction

Target cost is a key concept emphasized by many of the companies visited. This cost is driven by external market factors. One organization described it this way: "We examine the likely competitors and their products and then estimate the unit product cost necessary to be a viable entry in the market. This cost is labeled the target cost. We then work with the product engineers to see how we can design and produce a product at this target cost."

Japanese companies employ a target cost technique to reduce costs. Prior to designing a new product, a target cost is established, so that the product will be competitive after an introductory period at a certain production level. Engineers (who probably have spent time in manufacturing and accounting organizations) then design the product so that it can be made for the target cost. Once the target cost is achieved (possibly even earlier) a new, lower target cost is set. Engineering, manufacturing, and other departments then work together to meet the revised target cost. Japanese companies may, or may not, continually reduce prices to obtain market share as costs are reduced.

Investment Justification

The business environment in Japan encourages manufacturers to take a long-range view of operations; thus, it would be expected that they would be more likely than Western managers to invest in technology such as robotics, FMS, and CIM. But they have tended to use less sophisticated automation, such as pick-and-place robotics and refurbished equipment. It also seems that the measures Japanese managers apply to investment decisions are not based on the same hard, quantifiable calculations that a Western manager would use.

Of course, a major difficulty in comparing methods is to establish what is "the" Japanese method. For that matter, it is probably just as inaccurate to describe "the" American or "the" British approach. Japanese managers are no less profit-motivated than Western managers are, although Japanese managers probably feel less pressure for short-term results.

Investment Motivation

Investments in Japanese business are made mostly to achieve "strategy positioning." This means that a key criterion of justification is the ability to reach a product's target cost. Other such "soft metrics" include flexibility in production, better product quality, market share, market positioning, and cost reduction.

All the interviews conducted by the CAM-I team in Japan were marked by a lack of emphasis on the quantification of investment analysis. No one—including the university professors—referred to a hurdle rate, although some did say that discounted cash-flow analyses were used as part of the investment analysis process. In all cases, interviewees referred to computing a project's payback rate. Also, everyone agreed that the results of these financial calculations were secondary to strategic orientations.

Role of Target Cost in Investment

The Japanese emphasis on the target cost makes it convenient for managers to justify investment on the basis that the project will help achieve the target cost. In other words, it might be less important for a Japanese manager than for Western managers to show how depreciation, WIP reductions, throughput increase, and other factors affect the economics of acquiring a new piece of technology. Instead, the Japanese manager might demonstrate that the new technology will enable the product to be made at the target cost. Because the achievement of this cost is fundamental to the overall product strategy (in division, plant, company, and nation) separate, piecemeal justification is de-emphasized.

Reliance on the Namawashi Approach

In matters of strategy and investment, Japanese senior managers tend to rely heavily on analysis and agreement by lower-level managers. Consensus is reached through a number of meetings, at a considerable cost in time and effort. The practice of providing managers with a variety of experiences enhances this investment management approach. Research managers and accounting managers typically spend time in line-manufacturing positions, which provides them with a broad perspective of the appropriateness of a particular investment. Final approval by senior managers is more likely to depend on whether lower-level managers agree on the investment than on a computation of net present value.

COST REPORTING

It has been indicated that a major difference between Japanese and Western cost management methods is the Japanese reliance on *qualitative* rather than *quantitative* metrics. This section discusses how the Japanese use quantitative measures for cost accounting.

Cost Accounting Practices

Progress in Japanese cost accounting practices has been most obvious in cost planning, cost reduction, and cost control in the manufacturing sector. Several interviewees expressed concern about the limited progress made in these activities in the distribution and marketing sectors. Japanese managers take a plantwide, life-cycle view of cost accounting.

Cost Planning. This activity is undertaken before production begins (and, in some cases, before the production line is built). Plant engineers and product designers play important roles in cost planning. The aim is to design both product and production facility with an appropriate mix of cost, quality, deliverability, and flexibility. What is considered appropriate reflects top management's strategies.

Cost Reduction. This activity begins in both the preproduction and production stages of the product life cycle. At several Japanese plants, cost-reduction targets are set for each product, depending on its stage in the life cycle. For example, a product may have a cost-reduction target of 25 percent in its first year and 15 percent in its second year. Cost-reduction targets are more common in assembly and fabrication plants than in process plants.

At several companies, line workers were all members of cost-reduction circles that sought ways to achieve the cost-reduction targets. This reflects the Japanese *quality circle approach,* applied to cost accounting. Each year individual workers are required to submit a specific number of cost-reduction ideas to be discussed by the cost-reduction circle. At one public accounting firm, all members of the staff were also required to submit cost-reduction ideas to be discussed by members of a cost-reduction team.

Cost Control. This activity starts with production. The sources of information for cost-control activities include personal observation by production-line or office workers, plant managers, and office managers; financial performance measures (inventory turnover ratios, variances based on standard costs for materials, labor, and overhead); and nonfinancial performance measures (production lead time, setup time, percentage of product defects, schedule attainment). The consistent impression is that cost planning and cost reduction are pivotal activities in Japanese organizations. Consultants who have worked both in North America and in Japan report that Japanese companies devote more resources to cost-planning and cost-reduction activities than do North American managers.

Target Cost Versus Standard Cost

Target costs are conceptually different from standard costs. Standard costs are predetermined costs built up from an *internal analysis* by industrial engineers. Target costs are based on *external analysis* of markets and competitors. One consultant reported that several firms compute two separate variances, one comparing actual costs with target costs and another comparing actual costs with standard costs.

Influence of Tax System

Many observers attribute Japanese internal-accounting methods to the country's system of taxation. For example, the asset lives used by many firms for depreciable assets need not be the same as the assets' economic lives, because of tax guidelines. Examples of allowable useful lives include six years for electronic computers and eight years for patent rights. Japanese firms can use straight-line or declining-balance methods for ordinary depreciation.

Similarities to North American Companies

Internal accounting systems of many Japanese companies are quite similar to those found in North American companies.

Absorption Costing

Most firms use absorption costing. While special studies may be made to estimate fixed and variable costs, categorization of costs on a fixed versus a variable basis (as in variable or direct costing) are the exception rather than the norm.

Direct Labor

The most common allocation basis for factory overhead is direct labor. Typically, this means direct-labor hours rather than direct-labor cost. Many Japanese managers are aware that with increased automation in their plants, direct labor may not have a cause-and-effect relation with factory overhead. Nevertheless, they are reluctant to move quickly to change their current use of direct-labor hours. One plant manager noted these concerns about changing to machine hours as an allocation basis:

- In some areas of the plant, direct-labor costs are high, and creating a causal relation between overhead and direct-labor hours is still reasonable.
- There is little information on the complexities that may arise with the use of machine hours. The machines covered by each cost pool are not necessarily homogeneous. It would be necessary to decide how to weight the machine hours of each individual machine to develop an accurate allocation basis.
- Managers are very familiar with using direct-labor hours. There does not appear to be an urgent reason to make a change.

Labor Plus Factory Overhead as Conversion-Cost Pool

Several firms combine labor costs with factory overhead into a single conversion-cost pool when computing product costs. For these firms, labor costs were less than 10 percent of total manufacturing costs.

PERFORMANCE MEASUREMENT

Japanese managers apply different performance measures at different levels of management within a company.

Corporate (Top Company)

At the highest levels of management the difference between Japanese and Western performance measurement is characterized by the overall Japanese marketing strategy: focus on market share and growth rather than on profit or return-on-investment.

Division/Plant

At the middle levels of management Japanese managers use both financial and nonfinancial measures. Financial measures typically include total cost, meeting specific cost targets, and demonstrating cost improvement. Nonfinancial measures are often merely summaries of shop-floor measurements: lead time (days), quality, productivity, WIP, inventory turnover, and meeting production schedules.

Shop Floor

Japanese shop-floor measures are primarily physical. Managers apparently feel that conversion to financial measures would require too much effort when the physical measures are sufficiently understandable. These measures typically include meeting daily schedules, parts produced, hours worked, defects, and WIP inventory.

Performance Measurement Example

To illustrate Japanese performance measurement practices, consider the concepts used for the development cycle of a new car (see Table 9.1). The planning phase addresses the areas for continued performance improvement.

Table 9.1
Toyota Model (Planned Performance Improvements)

I	II	III	IV
Producibility	Safety	Riding comfort	Parts standard
High quality	Economy	Drivability	High-grade
Durability	Low emission	Comfort	Weight reduction
Reliability	Low noise	Maneuverability	Long life
Serviceability	Fuel saving	Easy to operate	Maintenance-free
Low cost	Resource savings	Wide inner space	Low price

Importance of Dynamic Measures

Managers also say they feel it is very important for performance measurements to measure those areas that are meaningful for current as well as for long-term perspectives.

INDUSTRY	PERSONS INTERVIEWED
Fuji Electric Company, Ltd.	Mr. Shinya Ueda, General Manager
Fuji Electric F.A. Engineering Company, Ltd.	Mr. Wataru Yuzawa, Director Mr. Takashi Kurihara, Vice President
Fujitsu Limited	Mr. Sadao Fujii, Manager
Ministry of Posts & Telecommunications	Mr. Masaaki Sakamaki, Senior Staff
Nippon Steel Corporation	Mr. Kuniichi Fujii, Asst. General Manager
Oki Electric Industry Company Ltd.	Mr. Hirokuni Takano, Staff Manager
Sharp Corporation	Mr. Issei Terashi, General Manager
Toshiba Corporation	Dr. Masaharu Kinoshita, Manager Mr. Eiichi Sano, Manager

ACCOUNTING/CONSULTING FIRMS	
Bain & Company Japan, Inc.	Mr. Jiro Sekine, Consultant
Chuo Coopers & Lybrand Consulting	Mr. Yoshiharu Hayakawa, CPA

Hong Kong Productivity Council	Dr. Daniel Doo, Consultant
Japan Information Service, Ltd.	Mr. Tetsuo Hashimoto, Manager
Peat, Marwick, Mitchell & Company	Mr. L. S. Miller, Managing Director
	Mr. Kenichi Takahashi, CPA
	Mr. William R. Sexsmith, Partner
Tohmatsu Awoki & Sanwa	Mr. Junichi Inque, CPA
	Mr. Naoko Hatakeyama, Consultant

ACADEMIC CONSULTANTS

Aoyama Gakuin University	Dr. Kenyo Kobayashi, Professor
Hitotsubashi University	Mr. Koyoshi Okamoto, Professor
Senshu University	Dr. Michiharu Sakurai, Professor
Waseda University	Dr. Jinishiro Nakane, Professor

GLOSSARY

Abandonment Analysis The process of determining if it is more profitable to continue or discontinue a product or project.

Acquisition Cost The cash or cash-equivalent value exchanged to acquire goods or services and have them available for use.

Activities Those actions required to achieve the goals and objectives of the function.

Activity Accounting The collection of financial and operational performance information about significant activities of the business.

AI See *Artificial Intelligence.*

Artificial Intelligence (AI) A branch of computer science that uses computer programs to solve problems that appear to require human deductive reasoning.

As Is The characteristics of the current system or operation.

Back flushing A costing system that focuses first on the throughput of an organization and then works backward when allocating costs between cost of goods sold and inventory.

Basic Research and Development Activities not linked to specific products, whose main function is to develop new product features and capabilities or to discover new manufacturing methods or technologies.

Bill of Material (BOM) A list of direct materials needed for the production of a given product.

BOM See *Bill of Material.*

Budget The quantification of the operating plan in dollars.

Budget Center The synonym for cost center during the budgeting or planning process.

Burden Rate See *Overhead Rate.*

CAD See *Computer-Aided Design.*

CAM See *Computer-Aided Manufacturing.*

CAM-I See *Computer Aided Manufacturing-International, Inc.*

Capacity The amount of labor or machine time needed to meet a schedule.

Capital Decay Lost sales due to technologically obsolete products and processes.

Carrying Charges Costs caused by work-in-process (WIP).

CAS See *Cost Accounting Standards.*

Chart of Accounts A list of accounts maintained by a specific enterprise.

CIM See *Computer-Integrated Manufacturing.*

CNC See *Computer Numerical Control.*

Computer-Aided Design (CAD) A type of engineering software that permits interactive development of a design, electronic blueprint, or visual representation of a manufacturing component or part on a video display terminal.

Computer-Aided Manufacturing (CAM) The use of computers to program, direct, and control production equipment in the fabrication of manufactured items.

Computer Aided Manufacturing-International, Inc. (CAM-I) A research consortium based in Arlington, Texas.

Computer-Integrated Manufacturing (CIM) The use of computers and various advanced manufacturing techniques to perform or assist in the activities necessary to manufacture an item.

Computer Numerical Control (CNC) A numerical control system where a dedicated computer is used to perform the numerical control functions.

Conceptual Design The formulation and general statement of a product's description.

Cost Accounting Standards (CAS) The nineteen standards developed by the Cost Accounting Standards Board to be followed when contracting with the government.

Cost Accounting System The system in an organization that provides for the collection and assignment of costs to intermediate and final cost objects.

Cost-Behavior Pattern Estimation of how costs behave as volume changes over a relevant range of activity levels.

Figure 1

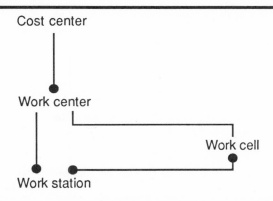

Cost Center The smallest unit of an organization for which budgeted or actual costs are collected and which has some common characteristics for measuring performance and assigning responsibility. A cost center can consist of one or more work centers, work cells, or work stations, as depicted in Figure 1.

Cost Driver A factor whose occurrence creates cost.

Cost Elements Types of costs (labor, material, service, supplies) associated with the manufacturing process.

Cost Factor A rate in dollars or percentages utilized to allocate or attach overhead cost to a product.

Cost of Quality The total expense incurred by a company to prevent poor quality, to evaluate quality, and to report internal and external product failures.

Cost Pools A grouping of indirect costs caused by the same cost drivers for the purpose of identification with or allocation to cost centers, processes, or products.

Current Standards The value associated with the current configuration and manufacturing process for a product.

Cycle Time The amount of time between the point when material for a product enters a factory and the point when the product is shipped.

DCF See *Discounted Cash Flow.*

Direct Cost A cost item that can be identified specifically with a single cost object in an economically feasible manner.

Direct Labor The cost of labor that can be directly identified with a specific product.

Direct Numerical Control (DNC) Refers to the operation of several numerical control machines directly from a single computer.

Discounted Cash Flow (DCF) A financial appraisal technique for comparing the returns of projects that differ with respect to the size of investment and the size and time of cash returns.

Distributed Numerical Control Data is sent from a main computer to a CNC system where it is stored, allowing the CNC system to now operate independently.

DNC See *Direct Numerical Control;* also *Distributed Numerical Control.*

Driver An activity or condition that has a direct influence on the operational performance and cost structure, or both, of other activities.

ECN See *Engineering Change Notice.*

Economic Order Quantity (EOQ) The number of units of inventory that should be ordered at one time in order to minimize the expected annual cost of the inventory system.

Engineering Change Notice (ECN) A written means of communicating that a revision has been made to either the product design or the manufacturing process. The engineering change notice may be predicated upon a customer request or an internal modification.

EOQ See *Economic Order Quantity.*

Expected/Projected Cost The anticipated cost of a specific product utilizing new assumptions identified after standard costs are set. The changes may include new volumes, bill-of-material change notices, or price updates.

Expert System A computer system with the ability to modify the program or data; it "learns by experience" and provides new solutions to developing situations.

Fixed Assets Noncurrent, nonmonetary, tangible assets used in normal operations of the business.

Fixed Costs 1. Operating costs that do not vary with changes in the level of activity over a relevant range of such activity. 2. Those costs that will be unaffected by variations in activity level in a given period.

Flexible Budget A plan that specifies the amount of cost for each item that should be incurred for any volume of production.

Flexible Manufacturing System (FMS) An integrated system of machine tools and material-handling equipment designed to manufacture a variety of parts at low or medium volumes.

FMS See *Flexible Manufacturing System.*

Function A group of activities having a common objective within the business.

Group Technology An engineering and manufacturing philosophy that identifies the "sameness" of parts, equipment, or processes.

Holding Costs The costs of holding an asset, including the cost of providing the capital invested in the asset, insurance, taxes, storage, and handling.

Indirect Costs 1. Costs common to a multiple set of cost objectives and not directly assignable to such objectives in a specific time period. Such costs are usually allocated by systematic and consistent techniques to products, processes, or time periods. 2. Costs that are not directly assignable/traceable to the product or process. 3. Expenses that do not have a close causal relation with the items being produced. These costs do not include the cost of service departments. An example of an indirect cost is production supplies not included in the bill of material.

In-Process Stores The storage of WIP inventory.

Investment Management Part of a product's process planning and development activity, because it directly affects the selection and acquisition of the technology used to make the product.

Islands of Automation Stand-alone automated processes (robotics, CAD/CAM, numerically controlled machines) without the integration required for a cohesive system.

JIT See *Just-in-Time.*

Just-in-Time (JIT) A logistics approach designed to result in minimum inventory and waste during the manufacturing process.

LAN See *Local Area Networks.*

Lead Time The span of time between the request for delivery of parts and their actual arrival.

Life-Cycle Costing Accumulation of costs for activities that occur over the entire life cycle of a product, from inception to abandonment by the manufacturer and the consumer.

"Lights Out" Factory A factory of the future where, it is implied, no manual labor exists—only automated equipment. The term suggests that once the factory has been started up on a cyclical basis, the lights could be turned out and the factory would still function.

Local Area Network (LAN) A vehicle, typically coaxial or fiber-optic cable, by which data can be transferred between system components that need to communicate.

Machine Hours The measurement of time used by a machine to monitor a specified level of output.

Make/Buy Decision The act of deciding whether to produce an item in-house or buy it from an outside vendor.

Management Information System (MIS) An organized method of providing past, present, and prospective information relating to internal operations and external intelligence. It supports the planning, controlling, and operational functions of an organization by providing information in the proper time frame to assist decision makers.

Market Research The collection and interpretation of information about markets, market trends, and customer preferences.

Master Production Schedule Requirements The application of sales forecasts (demand) and actual customer orders to internal resources to establish a schedule for producing the product.

Material-Requirements Planning (MRP) A system that translates a production schedule into net requirements for each component needed to meet the schedule.

MIS See *Management Information System.*

Move Time The actual time that a job spends in transit from one operation to another in the shop.

MRP See *Material-Requirements Planning.*

NC See *Numerically Controlled.*

Non-Value-Added Cost A cost or activity that can be eliminated with no deterioration of product attributes (e.g., performance, functionality, quality, perceived value) (see Table 1 at *Value-Added Cost*).

Numerically Controlled (NC) Refers to those machines that obtain instructions to perform an operation through a defined, machine-readable set of numeric codes representing specific actions.

"Off-Line" Quality Control Quality- and cost-control activities conducted during the product and process design stages to improve product manufacturability and reliability and to reduce life-cycle costs.

Operations Manufacturing activities in which work is performed on parts.

Optimized Manufacturing Optimal use of all pertinent tools and techniques to accomplish business goals or to perform an operation through a series of production steps called operations or processes. Costs are accumulated by those operations or processes for a specified time period; an average cost per unit of output is developed for costing purposes.

Overhead Rate The percentage rate at which overhead is applied to products.

Process Development Activities, such as planning, engineering, and technology selection, required to prepare the organization and the physical facility to release the product to production management.

Process Engineering Determination of the industrial, mechanical, and electrical engineering procedures for making the product.

Process Planning Activities necessary to classify the resources and operations employed in manufacturing (especially quality-control operations).

Product Costs Costs, including those for raw materials, direct labor, and technology, that are directly or indirectly involved in the production of goods and services for sale to customers. Indirect costs include such items as equipment maintenance, factory utilities, and wages for facilitating services in the plant. Indirect costs are customarily assigned to products or services by an appropriate allocation technique.

Product Development All activities required to define, design, develop, test, release, and maintain the complete description of the products to be manufactured.

Production Monitoring An activity that provides dynamic status information of production activities.

Production Planning and Control System A system that ensures a balance between resources and requirements.

Production Programming The creation and maintenance of programs (software) used in production, including such areas as NC, CNC, DNC, and robotics.

Project Management Scheduling and organizational activities to control production.

Pull System The production of items only as demanded for use or to replace those taken for use.

Quality-Control Activities Checking, physical inspection, gauging, and testing done with the product.

Rework Cost Model A parameter-driven quality model that determines whether a part should be reworked or scrapped.

Rework/Repair Manufacturing resources consumed to bring a substandard part up to standard.

Scrap The number of units started in an operation that are later judged unusable.

Service/Support Center A work center whose primary mission is to provide specialized support to other departments.

Setup The process of preparing a machine or work center for a manufacturing process.

Shop-Floor Control A work unit that includes people employed to strike a balance between resources and requirements.

Standard Costs Normally, the annual process of calculating the anticipated cost of a specific product at a given level of volume and under an assumed set of circumstances.

Strategic Planning A planning process that summarizes and articulates the basic operational tasks, objectives, goals, and strategies for the organization.

Sunk Costs Costs that have been incurred, but not consumed, for generating future revenue.

System Design Production of a functional prototype design.

Taguchi Method A strategy of quality improvement focused on removing the effects of causes rather than the cause.

Target Cost A market-based cost that is calculated using a sales price necessary to capture a predetermined market share. Target cost = Sales price (for the target market share) − Desired profit.

Task Work element of an activity.

Technology Cost The purchase price, startup cost, interest, current market value adjustment, and risk premium of an acquisition.

Throughput The total volume of production through a facility (machine, work center, department, plant).

Time Charging A reporting system that tracks labor by task and flags shortfalls due to absences.

To Be The proposed characteristics of a system or operation.

Tolerance Design A design that determines the amount of control the

Table 1

DIRECT LABOR $= 8$ HOURS	
VALUE-ADDED	NON-VALUE-ADDED
1. Assemble	1. Waiting
2. Pack	2. Walking

PURCHASING $= 8$ HOURS	
VALUE-ADDED	NON-VALUE-ADDED
1. Order material	1. Expedite
2. Negotiate savings	2. Revise purchase order

manufacturer will have over the parameters (and hence, over loss and quality).

Tooling The defining, procuring, storing, maintaining, inspecting, delivering, repair, and calibration of the physical tools required in production.

Total Quality Control A management strategy in which all business functions work together to build quality into the products.

TQC See *Total Quality Control.*

Transactions Physical (including electronic) documents associated with activities that impact information.

Value-Added Cost The incremental cost of an activity to complete a required task at the lowest overall cost (see Table 1).

Variable Cost 1. A cost that increases as the volume of activity increases and decreases as the volume of activity decreases. 2. Those costs that are affected by the level of activity in a period.

Waste The net of total process output minus good process output.

Whole-Life Cost The cost to the customer from product inception to abandonment.

WIP See *Work-in-Process.*

WIP/Queue-Related Material Movement Affects materials related to in-process backlogs.

Work Cell A grouping of individuals or machines that perform a job or process.

Work Center A specific area of the factory or company, consisting of one or more people or machines, where a particular product or process is performed. A work center may consist of one or more work cells or work stations.

Work Station A location where an individual worker performs a job.

Working Capital 1. The excess of current assets over current liabilities. 2. Sometimes used to mean current assets, when the excess of current assets over current liabilities is referred to as net working capital.

Work-in-Process (WIP) The investment in goods in the process of being produced.

Yield The difference between input and output of a process.

INDEX

BOLD numbers refer to glossary pages.